D0016799

The Focinar℠

(FOH-kin-are)

A Genuine Persuasion System

by John L. Evans, Jr.

The Focinar

First Edition

Printed in the United States of America

ISBN 97809778863-0-2: $14.95

Library of Congress Control Number: 2006923659

THIS BOOK IS DEDICATED TO

Uncle Rowly

JOURNALIST AND PATRIOT

Special thanks to
David Larrabee and David Keefer
for their help in bringing
this book to life.

"Where our work is, there let our joy be."

Tertullian

Foreword

My colleague, John L. Evans, brings to life an innovative, powerful concept in The Focinar: Sales professionals from all industries can indeed find joy in their work, achieve financial success, and add lasting benefits to their clients' lives if they change the way they do business. The gains are potentially limitless, and the process starts with you. When asked, "What do you want out of your sales career," how do you respond? Most likely you say passion, monetary success, and knowing that you are making a difference in the world. The Focinar will lead you there.

Aristotle said, "Pleasure in the job puts perfection in the work." Are you having fun at work? You might think that sounds too good to be true. But it is one of the biggest keys to your success, and when you use the principles of The Focinar, you will understand why. Think about your favorite hobbies, such as golfing, fishing, gardening, music, or wine. When we have a

Small opportunities are often the beginning of great enterprises.

Demosthenes

Money is better than poverty, if only for financial reasons.

Woody Allen

passion for something, we spend time perfecting our knowledge and performance, and ultimately the experience. The Focinar will help you surround yourself with the people and activities you enjoy the most. That will bring pleasure to your work, and rewards aplenty.

Without question, a successful professional services career should be financially rewarding. If yours isn't, something is wrong. Woody Allen joked, "Money is better than poverty, if only for financial reasons." When it comes to your career, the joke should never be on you. The Focinar can help you, or any sales professional, earn an exceedingly comfortable living. The rewards, however, will not magically appear. Getting there may require a sea change in your thinking. Your career is about you, but not only you. Indeed, to push your career as a sales professional to the next level, you must put others first.

When asked what he thought of Western civilization, Gandhi quipped,

"I think it would be a good idea." My favorite thing about the principles in this book is that they create civilized interaction, and that's a win-win, not a win-lose. Relying on these principles, sales professionals in any industry can help themselves by helping others first. And, oh, what joy comes from seeing our friends and trusted colleagues become successful, particularly when we have been instrumental in making it happen. As our clients become our "composers," as you will learn later in the book, we become blessed, relishing the symphony.

I am convinced this book can summon the very best in you and help you deliver just what your clients need.

May the Focinars begin!

Anastasia Rock
Vice President of Integrated Marketing
American Century Investments

Contents

The Focinar

My name is Larry Biederman. Author John L. Evans, Jr. likes to call me his mentor. I am not sure I deserve such high praise. But I am sure that the innovative ideas in this book can dramatically alter the careers of sales veterans, small-business owners, and professional service people of all stripes. My career proves it.

Like many young folks, I started with hopes and dreams of financial success but with very little in worldly possessions. It was 1965 and I was 27-year-old broker at Merrill Lynch. I had a wife, two children, a 12-year-old Chevy, and $35 in the bank. I desperately needed to succeed.

Early in my career my office manager pointed to the Columbus, Ohio, phone book and assured me that if I made 100 cold calls a day, I was sure to hit it big. Since he signed the paychecks, I heeded his advice and spent Monday through Friday and four nights a week for two months calling perfect strangers, asking them to invest with me. As you might expect, the rejection rate was close to 100 percent. After making thousands of calls, I had opened just one account — an elderly widow had $700 to invest.

Fortunately, the most successful broker in the office took notice of my hard work and growing frustration. Inviting me to lunch one day, he asked a simple question: "Who are you trying to do business with?" I answered, "anyone." He said, "if you try to do business with anyone, that's just who you'll get —

anyone." It was a foolish way to work. Instead, he urged me to focus my efforts on three niche markets — niches with clients who I knew had money to invest. He asked me to tell him at lunch that day just whom I would target. I decided to focus on doctors. It was my first introduction to focused marketing, the principles that John L. Evans, Jr. explains with passion in The Focinar.

If you chase two rabbits, both will escape.

Anonymous

After just eight days, my focused efforts started to bear fruit. I opened an account with a wealthy doctor and wrote my first 1,000-share order. It was a start, and when I proceeded to ask the doctor for advice on how to grow my business, he told me exactly how to meet other wealthy doctors practicing in the same hospital. I didn't know it at the time, but I had stumbled upon a piece of wisdom that I later learned from Dr. Charles Dwyer, an expert on persuasion: Asking for advice is the "number one way to positively influence another person."

These two simple ideas — focused marketing and asking for advice — helped me develop a brokerage practice in just two years that exceeded all industry averages and ranked in the top 2 percent of my peer group at Merrill Lynch.

The most important single central fact about a free market is that no exchange takes place unless both parties benefit.

Milton Friedman

In 1970, I became a manager with the firm and used these techniques to help hundreds of financial advisors grow their careers. Some of their success stories are truly heartwarming. One advisor, who had never climbed out of the basement in 29 years, increased his production by 300 percent in two years and qualified for a top recognition club at Merrill Lynch. At an awards event, his wife tearfully thanked me for changing their lives. Wow.

I retired from the firm in 1998, but I just couldn't put the lessons I learned on the shelf. So I helped start a training and consulting firm, PSBtraining.com, and created a program entitled SMARTMarketing that's based on focused marketing and the advice process. Since 1999, my partners and I have taught the techniques in every major national and regional financial services firm. New and experienced advisors have used SMARTMarketing to dramatically expand their practices. By putting the program to work, one young lion at a southeastern firm boosted his commissions from $25,000 in 2002 to more than $800,000 in 2005.

John L. Evans, Jr. captures the essence of focused marketing and the advice process, describing them in entertaining and edifying terms. Whether you are a new persuasion executive or a sales veteran, a small-business owner or a lawyer, banker, or doctor, I promise you that implementing these techniques will help you make more money and have more fun in your professional and personal life. So please do me one favor: After you read the book, get started right away. You will be thrilled with the results.

Good luck.

Larry Biederman

Founder, PSBTraining.com

Editor's Note

To maximize the value of this book, a persuasion executive must learn its unique language. First and foremost, the reader must understand the word "Focinar" (FOH-kin-are). It might sound strange at first — it's not a real word, after all. But that makes perfect sense. The concepts in this book are a little unusual, even unsettling, and the word "Focinar" reflects that brand of innovative thinking. When a persuasion executive is getting nowhere with antiquated marketing techniques, he needs to be innovative in order to change his luck. Learning the language of the Focinar, also known as "focinese," is a first step. The Glossary in the back of the book can help. Please refer to it as often as necessary.

Adam J. Martin

"So I saw that there is nothing better for people than to be happy in their work. That is why they are here!"

King Solomon

Introduction

Designed for all professional service people and small-business owners, this is a "Selling 201" book from the course that was never offered to you in school. If you have had any formal sales training, more than likely it was from a business manager who was lackluster at the craft. This book will take you places you have never been. It is about creating and retaining your unassailable competitive advantage. It is for anybody who is paid, or held accountable, for effective persuasion.

This book will take you places you have never been.

Albert Einstein said that things should be as simple as possible, but no simpler. As a persuasion executive, you are looking for the most seamless, efficient approach to growing your business with the best clients available. This book will ask you to sit down and have one conversation with each of your 10 best clients. I am going to explain a system for these conversations that has a proven track record of success. I am going to tell you when and how to execute these conversations so that they lead, quite naturally, to an event that will change your life. This event is what I call the "Focinar" (FOH-kin-are).

Think focused seminar, where you sell one-on-one to a group of like-minded people.

Think focused seminar, where you sell one-on-one to a group of like-minded people. A Focinar is one-on-one because all your audience members have similar needs. So even though you may be talking to a group during this seminar, it feels as if you're talking to an individual.

If you correctly execute the conversations with your 10 best clients, you can expect to experience four remarkably valuable business responses, each of which leads to a Focinar. That's batting .400 — Ted Williams territory. If you do not feel your business batting average is comparable to that of Mr. Williams, I think you will find this book valuable. And the best part is, it requires no heavy lifting. I will ask you only to make some simple adjustments in your interactions with your best clients. There are no spreadsheets, software installations, or wardrobe enhancements.

Introduction

The Focinar is the most powerful tool for business development I have experienced in my 15 years in national politics and business. Yes, the immediate focus at this seminar is on the needs of potential clients, but I describe the Focinar as life-changing because the ultimate focus is on your professional success and personal well-being. Expect outstanding results from the Focinar.

I am a sales executive for American Century Investment Services, one of the premier investment managers in the world. Fortune magazine has ranked American Century as one of the best firms to work for at least seven years in a row. I am deeply grateful for American Century's support in making this book a reality, and sincerely hope it contributes to the betterment of your business practice.

Chaucer said at the beginning of Canterbury Tales, "As we are all pilgrims journeying to Canterbury individually, why not walk together and tell each other our stories?" As a persuasion executive, this is my story of what works. I welcome your stories as well.

Now let's get started on our journey.

Section 1

"Yee above and below
the art of persuasion,
accept my gratitude...
The bounty increaseth
for the rest."

Nicholas Fontaigne

The Problems

Admit it: Many of your clients drive you completely out of your mind.

Let's keep it real right from the get-go of this book. Far too many of your clients sap the life out of you. They do next-to-nothing for the health of your business and your personal well-being. What's more, you simply tolerate many other clients who aren't particularly dislikeable but show no inclination to stick with you. A sales professional living a quiet life of desperation, you are probably just going through the motions with many in your book of business. I don't care if you are selling investment services, legal services, insurance products, accounting services, pharmaceuticals, real estate, or pet rocks. More than likely, this is your reality.

This book asks why, offers an insightful answer, and proposes a solution that can change your life. My belief is that a demoralizing ennui paralyzes a sales professional after four or five years on the job. It's an ennui born of settling for

The greatest discovery of my generation is that a human being can alter his life by altering his attitude.

William James

mediocrity. It's a feeling of powerlessness, of futility. I have seen it happen to innumerable colleagues during my time in national politics, medical sales, and investment services. I have seen it happen to the hundreds of sales professionals I have consulted. It just kind of creeps up on you, like a slow fog, drifting into your business life, stymieing your professional joie de vivre. At first it's just a nuisance. But if you don't address the problem, it gets worse, until one day, horror of horrors, the alarm clock activates, and you simply cannot get out of bed to go see that knucklehead client one more time.

The origin of the problem is weak academic and professional training. The foundation of sales is persuasion, but higher institutions do not routinely teach persuasion, and you are unlikely to learn the art and science of persuasion from some connect-the-dots corporate lesson plan. Yet, if we are judged by what we contribute to the world, what could be more important than learning how to be effective at persuasion? Think of the most influential people ever to walk the Earth: Jesus, Buddha, Mohammed, and Martin Luther come to mind. Jesus persuaded others on the value of forgiveness, Buddha on patience, Mohammed on trust, Luther on reform. History is clear about how effective they were at persuasion.

I have no interest in bashing managers. As a matter of fact, I have great respect for the arduous tasks of successful management. But let's face it: Management is typically woeful when it comes to teaching persuasion. Management and selling are distinct skills, and most sales professionals instinctively know the difference. You undoubtedly have had to endure far too many insufferable meetings led by a manager who couldn't persuade a college music major to purchase an iPod. We all know that we learn best from our peers, not from pointy-headed know-it-alls. It is a principle perhaps best seen on the baseball field, a microcosm of life. The best players do most of their learning from other players. Dante Bichette, who made a number of appearances in major-league all-star games, tells me that learning about hitting is done "around the batting cage with other guys" before games. This book aims to be your batting cage before the big game called your career. I will introduce you to a number of the "other guys," regular persuasion executives, though largely Google-free, who are taking their businesses to extraordinary places. I will illuminate their most important strategies — and show you how to go from an unreliable, unmotivated singles hitter to a perennial all-star.

The most valuable players in the world of persuasion don't rely on the antiquated marketing techniques still being taught in the academy and corporate conference rooms. The reason is simple: That kind of training has not advanced in corresponding fashion with the revolution in commerce. With the Internet and the astounding velocity at which information moves now, a sustainable competitive advantage is a dinosaur. Today, virtually all of us are selling commodities. As a persuasion executive, you probably feel that your client could walk to a competitor in a New York minute and there wouldn't be much you could do; the client's needs would still be met, just by someone other than you.

More than likely you have experienced that disquieting sensation when competitors have successfully copycatted your firm's latest innovation, at warp factor 5. Now try falling back on your lackluster training, and that sensation only gets worse. Irrespective of which line of persuasion you're in, managers still teach antiquated marketing techniques (like cold calling, letter writing, and simply asking for referrals) with disappointing regularity. These approaches are like Model-Ts in today's Indy 500 economy. The worst marketing approach of all time is the "Sit and Swivel" — the persuasion executive just sits around and waits for accounts from the "munificent" manager or principal. As crazy as that sounds, "Sit and Swivel" is common in accounting, law, and finance. But it is not a strategy. After "Sit and Swivel," you might as well focus on "hocus-pocus" marketing strategies. It's all borderline madness. My friend and mentor, Larry Biederman, explains it this way: You do the same old marketing stuff and expect different results. There is the source of your quiet desperation.

Be honest: Business as usual leads to disappointing results. If most of your clients drive you out of your mind, yet you stick with antiquated strategies, over time 10 percent of your clients will end up generating 90 percent of your business. In my experience the old "80/20 rule" is more like the "90/10 rule." Unless you change your ways, 90 percent of your clients will contribute close to 100 percent of the funk that leads to your eventual alarm clock paralysis. Do you believe the prominent financial services consultant who counsels, "Just one more call over time will yield so much more business?" That's hooey these days. Late-night cold calling only serves to chill the sales professional's spouse, who sits at home alone. And a late-night cold call is never as lucrative as you might hope. That call has a 1 in 10 chance of yielding a desirable client. Bad odds.

It's choice – not chance – that determines your destiny.

Jean Nidetch

Section 1

Like the golfer in the illustration, you need the right club to hit the green. So what is the alternative to cold calling, to those antiquated marketing strategies, to the same old malarkey?

You may not believe it now, but you do have an alternative. How do I know? I live it. My present approach is infinitely more rewarding and durable than anything I tried earlier in my career. I have seen my income increase significantly using a technique that I promise you can master. Equally important, my quality of life and sustainability as a persuasion executive have radically improved.

Initially, like every other fledgling persuasion account manager, I went down the original marketing road, scratching and clawing my way toward a bigger book of business. I hoped to find new clients using what I had been taught, but I was banging away with THE WRONG golf club. In hindsight, the outcomes were predictable: My income was OK, but the funk got up on me.

Like me, you need the right golf club in your hands. Once it is there, I am confident you will hit the green time and time again. You will acquire the right kind of clients, the ones you cannot find enough of right now. Your life will get better. It is that simple.

In the graph on the following page, called your "Funk-Adjusted Returns" SM (F.A.R.), I will illustrate what you can achieve. The vertical axis represents your returns — but not just the monetary rewards you bring home. I mean your income multiplied by the joy you achieve from making a contribution to the marketplace — and the welfare of others. The horizontal axis represents your "funk." By funk, I mean any undesirable experiences that must be endured to have success — such as spending time away from family and loved ones, playing energy-sapping corporate politics, managing knucklehead colleagues who smile at the boss while barking at the administrative assistant, or slogging through start-up challenges. The more of these experiences you endure, the worse your funk. (One of my

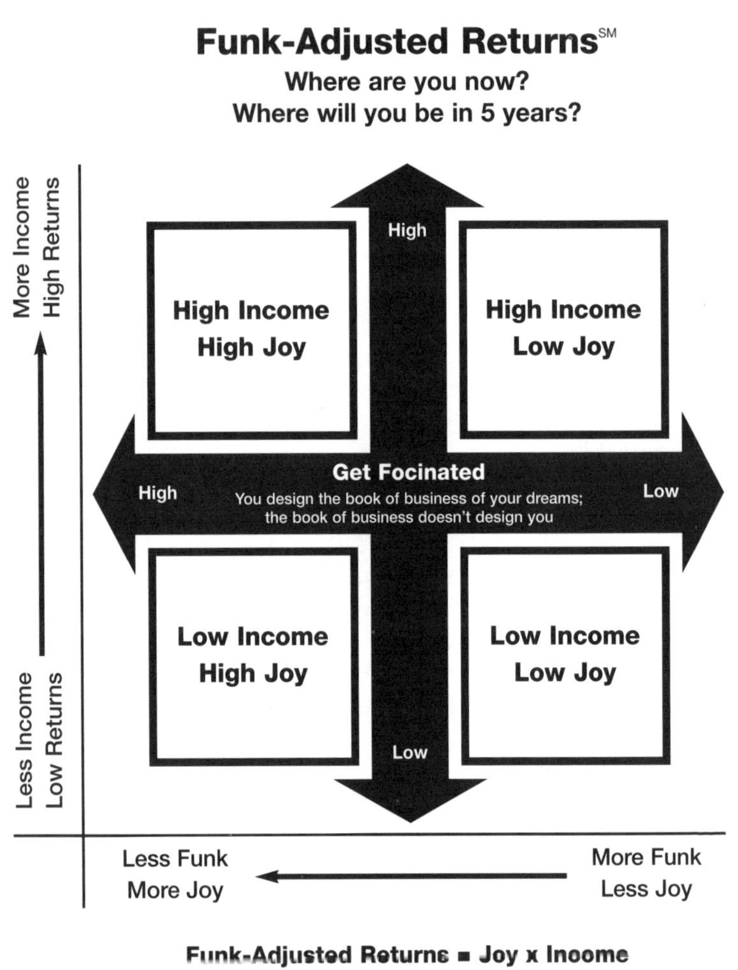
Funk-Adjusted Returns℠
Where are you now?
Where will you be in 5 years?
More Income
High Returns
Less Income
Low Returns
High
Low
High Income
High Joy
High Income
Low Joy
Low Income
High Joy
Low Income
Low Joy
Get Focinated
High
Low
You design the book of business of your dreams;
the book of business doesn't design you
Less Funk
More Joy
More Funk
Less Joy
Funk-Adjusted Returns = Joy x Income
(from contribution to ideal clients)

operating premises: Increased time spent with family and close friends will automatically reduce your funk.) Your ideal destination on the graph is the top left: maximum returns, minimal funk.

An extreme example may be helpful. If you had a rich uncle whom you adored, and you happened to give him an idea for a breakthrough left-handed wrench, and he returned a year later with a $10 million check for you, your Funk-Adjusted Returns for that endeavor would be as high as can be: top left. You earned a huge chunk of change. You made an enormous contribution to the quality of your beloved uncle's life. And you forfeited no time away from family. Tremendous returns, with zero accompanying time and pain.

Another example: You have a brilliant idea for a new horse carriage. You borrow money up to your eyeballs, work 70 hours a week, and become fully engaged as an entrepreneur. Every week you have to answer to your lenders. Your husband leaves you because you have abandoned the family in exchange for work. You are just about to receive your first purchase order when you open the newspaper and observe the announcement of this new invention called the automobile. Your deal collapses. What accrues to you? Nothing but zero returns and immense stress.

To get where you want to go — to maximize your F.A.R.— you may have to go far, metaphorically speaking. Imagine the graph is actually a map of this great nation. No doubt you have traveled all over the map in your career. In the first example above, the idea you shared with your beloved uncle earned you a no-pain, big-gain trip to Seattle, the top left corner of the map. But all that sweat equity you expended and real debt you incurred in hopes of hitting it big on a horse carriage landed you in a South Florida hothouse, the bottom right corner of the map. (No offense is directed here at the good people of Miami and the good times anyone can enjoy in that tropical part of the country. Remember: This is a metaphor.) In Boston, the top right, perhaps you are a successful investment banker, working 70 hours a week, sporting a pair of golden handcuffs. Your returns are great, but only at the expense of your personal life. I have a name for this individual - Elliot Funkhauser. In San Diego, perhaps you are a struggling artist, delighting your small band of clients and enjoying your family, but living on a less-than-titillating income. Your goal, wherever you are now, is to head toward Seattle.

Here's how. I submit to you, with unadulterated zeal, shouting at the top of my lungs, from the tallest mountain outside Seattle, naked in the sunshine, that the surefire way to move northwestwardly — to maximize your Funk-Adjusted Returns — is to increase your number of truly ideal clients. The clients you love. You know them: When they walk into your office, both of you alight. It is a feeling down at the cellular level. You both feel genuine caring and mutual respect. You ask

Don't be Elliot!

about her family, and you genuinely care about her family. You both connect — and life is richer.

The wonderful rewards you reap from these relationships seem all the more amazing in light of your hassle-filled experiences with a knucklehead client. You endure the indignity of his consistent mispronouncing of your name. He does not get off his can to greet you — you are persona non grata. His first utterance is about price. His second is a declaration that you will be sponsoring him at his next whatever event. Perhaps he will even fire off a deep groin scratch just as you are about to ask for his business. Gross. You get an eerie feeling that he would not

Ten percent of your clients typically deliver 90 percent of your business.

hesitate to pick up the blower and call your boss to complain about the tiny stain on your tie. I once had a client send back my gift of golf balls, insisting he only plays with Callaway. The nerve of that barbarian.

I do not care if you are a derivatives trader trying to find more ideal clients for your hedge fund-of-funds, an accountant trying to take your business to the next level, or a dry cleaner. The one question central to your career and your life is, "How do I get more ideal clients?" By the way, do not settle for less, and from this point forward, make it your active aim never to settle again.

Remember the 90/10 rule? Ten percent of your clients typically deliver 90 percent of your business. Now apply that rubric to the number of client relationships you manage in a typical year. It has been my experience that a persuasion executive will have somewhere between 50 and 1,000. The 90/10 rule says that executive will have only about 10 relationships that butter his bread. I am talking about the truly ideal clients. You know them. They stand out. You could reel off 35 facts on each one of them in a minute. I want you to think of these clients — your best 10 relationships — as your composers. Why? They are composing the symphony called your business. Composers have vision and passion — qualities essential to the success of any enterprise. Their value to you is infinite. If you lost one, it would hurt emotionally and financially.

Are you unsure of your composers' identities? According to Gallup Research, one in every 10 customers in every industry, from retail to banking, is passionate. These are your composers. Here is a handy trick: Rate every one of your clients on a scale of 1 to 10 in two metrics. First, rank them by how much you like them — one is unbearable, 10 is you love them. Second, rank each one by how much business they deliver to you. One is very little, 10 is as much as you want. Now grab your calculator and multiply the scores. The clients who rate 90 and above hold the keys to that luxury sedan headed for Seattle. They are not only great clients in the present; they are your future. They form the cornerstone of this book, and I want you to think of the value in these relationships as equity you have earned.

Section 2

“The advice of the wise is like a life giving fountain... Those who accept it avoid the snares of death.”

Proverbs 13

The Value of Advice

Your 10 best clients, your composers, can do so much for you. But far too often they are an underutilized lot in your book of business. Like thoroughbreds, they are just starving to get out of the gates on your behalf. But often persuasion execs like you and me are just too busy telling stories when we see these clients, making sure they are getting the latest brochure on the super widget, or just truly enjoying each other's company, that we miss the opportunity to run with them to the winner's circle. We might remember to ask for a referral, and often they oblige. That's nice. But you sense down deep that they could do a lot more for you.

I love hearing speakers on the topic of persuasion, and one day years ago I heard a one-hour presentation that changed my thinking about my composers — and my career. I was thunderstruck. The speaker was Charles Dwyer, PhD, an associate professor of philosophy and

If we are together, nothing is impossible. If we are divided, all will fail.

Winston Churchhill

education at the University of Pennsylvania. A renowned expert on human influence, Dr. Dwyer, in a sizzling, un-academic manner, preached about the number one way to positively influence another human being: by asking for that person's advice. Huh? What was that, Doc? If I want another person to do something truly valuable for me, I should ask for his advice? That's right: According to Dr. Dwyer, the best way to make a major impression on another person — on a client, for instance — is to seek his or her counsel. This sounded revolutionary to me, and I knew it might change my life as a persuasion professional.

When we ask for advice, we are usually looking for an accomplice.

Saul Bellow

But I did not know how, or how much, until I met Professor Roger Fisher, Director of the Harvard Negotiation Project and a renowned negotiation genius. While we took in a spring-training baseball game one afternoon in Sarasota, Florida, Dr. Fisher told me stories about how getting someone's advice can be such a powerful way to achieve mutual gains.

Recently in his office he pulled out a newspaper with the picture of one of his former students, the president of Paraguay, in a meeting with another dignitary. Professor Fisher actually chuckled and said, "The president is literally doing the advice method in this very meeting!"

Professor Fisher and Dr. Dwyer are persuasion pioneers. Their method — asking for advice when you are trying to influence another human being — is the first step you will take when you begin a conversation with one of your 10 best clients. The Fisher/Dwyer advice process is diametrically opposite to the experience of having to endure the following unsolicited line from practically anybody: "Let me give you some advice, young lady...."

Let's take Johnny, my 8-year old, to illustrate the power of the Fisher/Dwyer method. Admittedly, this is a simplistic example, but I offer it as an illustration of the sheer power that one person, no matter his station, can have over others. Johnny wanted his first BB gun, in a big way. So we had a chat, and I coached him to pose the following question to his mother, my wife, on the subject. "Mommy, please give me some advice. What would it take for me to get you comfortable enough to allow me to use my hard-earned money to purchase my first NRA-certified BB gun?" Not insignificantly, he asked the question just after doing a magnificent job at cleaning the dishes. There was a huge silence as my wife mulled it over.

This particular silence, incidentally, can be golden. Alyson's thinking was changing. There was a tectonic shift going on in her mind that would lead to Johnny's success.

"It would take 3 things," Alyson said:

- You take a gun safety course
- You only shoot in our back yard wearing protective eyewear at my pre-determined inanimate targets
- If you make so much as one infraction with the gun (point it at a sibling, for instance, or leave it lying around), the gun will be confiscated by me FOREVER

Eureka! Johnny struck gold. All he had to do was execute his mother's advice, and he would get his first BB gun! He took the course, passing it with flying colors, and is extremely diligent with his gun. Alyson, his mom, had no chance: As soon as she answered his question, satisfying his request for advice, she was a willing partner in the deal. She had been successfully and ethically persuaded to agree to her son's request.

Dr. Dwyer's and Professor Fisher's research was profound, with momentous implications for persuasion executives. My career is filled with proof that the Fisher/Dwyer method works wonders.

"So how do you suggest we proceed?" asked the United States Senator. He posed the question to a key constituent, hoping for advice about winning fundraising dollars from a prestigious "breakfast club" of C.E.O.s. At the time, I had no idea what my boss was doing. When the constituent, Tom, responded by saying that he would set up a dinner with the executives, I suddenly got it. Tom continued by saying he would furnish a set of talking points specifically tailored for the senator to deliver to the executives. The event was a home run. The senator ultimately was re-elected. Tom won a battle for our campaign. Amazing. The professors are right!

Years later I was working for Xymogen, a medical sales firm. One of my best clients was a brilliant, young neurologist from Naples, Florida, named David Perlmutter. Using our company's protocols and products, Dr. Perlmutter was getting some fantastic results with patients presenting with early-stage Parkinson's disease. He was quite enthusiastic about the results. As the relationships manager, I wanted him to spread the good word about his success. So I asked him, "How should we get this word out?" His response (and

The only thing to do with good advice is to pass it on.

Oscar Wilde

Doing things for others always pays dividends.

Claude M. Bristol

you will find this is not an atypical answer to the question): "I'll tell you how we are going to proceed in spreading this exciting success. We'll put on a seminar right here in beautiful Naples, and I will invite my colleagues from all around the Southeast. I'll focus on these protocols for Parkinson's." Oh, yeah! That seminar continues on, occurring annually. Xymogen's revenue and earnings continue to soar.

Recently, something marvelous happened for one of my clients. Chris, an emerging star at Ameriprise Financial (formerly American Express Financial Advisors), wanted to influence one of his own best clients because he wanted more just like her. His client was the head coach for a major university's women's basketball program. Chris executed the Fisher/Dwyer method, asking the head coach for advice on how to grow his financial advice business. After a dramatic pause, the coach said, "I'll tell you what we are going to do to grow your business. Next month I am throwing a party for many of the head coaches at the university; why don't you come, and I will introduce you as our personal advisor." Oh, yeah! By focusing on one type of client — head coaches — Chris made the event a huge success. His business continues to thrive today because of that one question for the coach. That is the power of the Fisher/Dwyer method. To build your book of business, you must strike up a conversation with your best clients. You start that conversation by asking for advice.

I tell these stories from the disparate worlds of politics, medicine, and finance because the truth is that the profession is unimportant. In each case, the stories have something in common. Yes, in each case, advice was requested. But that was only the start. Ultimately, all the stories resulted in an event. Ladies and gentlemen, they all concluded with a Focinar. Think focused seminar. The word spontaneously erupted out of a conversation I had with a promising young executive at Raymond James Financial Services, Todd Fosnow, and it made total sense.

Inspired out of the advice process, a Focinar is an event at which a group of like-minded individuals gather to hear a polished sales pitch — a customized value proposition. It's a focused seminar because you are going to dial in to the needs of your attendees. The Focinar is the fuel for your journey to

If you want to build the book of business of your dreams, you are going to have to change your behavior.

Seattle. When you put Focinars into action, you can expect increased income and an improvement in the quality of your clients. These events are more powerful than any cold call will ever be. They will generate the only kind of clients you really want, irrespective of your persuasion endeavor.

Remember, the rules of persuasion (or call it sales, if you like) have changed with the mass commoditization of goods and services. No longer can professionals simply grab their bag, sit in front of the prospect, and spew out some company line born out of the imagination of some power-starved bureaucrat back at the home office. No, if you want to build the book of business of your dreams, you are going to have to change your behavior. Otherwise, to draw on a baseball analogy, the ball (book of biz) is playing you. This will lead to an undesirable situation at some point, an error.

Here is an exercise I want you to try. For the next week, compile a list of your 10 best clients. Imagine how delightful life would/will be with 50 more of these folks! Or 100! Imagine the thrill of being in a position to fire that knucklehead client who unremittingly carps about price the instant you walk into the room. Perhaps you are an attorney, and you are just sick and tired of seeing that competitor on the billboard, gobbling up market share. You want something better. In fact, I do not care what line of business you are in — law, finance, small business, or something grander — you want more high-quality clients. So get the list done by next week, if it even takes that long. As you read on, you'll learn about the magic in that list — and what to do next.

Drive thy business or it will drive thee.

Benjamin Franklin

Section **3**

“Stay Hungry”

Steve Jobs

Commencement address, June 2005

Developing a Focinarket

What do you have passion for? What really gets you going, beyond just dollars? What would you be doing if you knew you could not fail? Whatever your response, it should be tethered to the place or space where you do business like nobody else on Earth. I call this space your focinarket, or focused market. This is where you can earn a life that is way beyond success; it could be the opportunity to earn a life of significance.

What would you be doing if you knew you could not fail?

To escape the rapacious jaws of commoditization, you simply must have a segment in the marketplace that you love and dominate. My mentor, Larry Biederman, always says that the only thing that cannot be commoditized these days is your knowledge about your clients and your personal market. Remember Chris, the financial advisor who works with NCAA coaches? He always wanted to be a coach himself; he loves coaching. He jumps out of bed like a panther to go to work because he feels he is making a contribution to his

The first step to getting the things you want out of life is this: Decide what you want.

Ben Stein

focinarket, which is college coaches. Using his knowledge of capital markets, he loves making their lives better.

My client Frank has done wonders tethering his passion for tennis to his focinarket. Frank has played some professional tennis, so he knows plenty about issues of concern to pro tennis players — the nature of compensation, the tour schedule, endorsements, etc. As a wealth manager for a major securities firm, he built his business around the sport he loves. I finally got him to agree to try the Fisher/Dwyer method, which took some effort, because he is a self-described proud man. Finally, he invited one of his composers — a tennis professional who had tasted decent material success, but no great repute — to Starbucks and asked for her advice about how he could grow his business with other successful tennis pros. Frank had recently helped the composer's mother with a crucial inheritance decision. Faced with Frank's question, the composer paused, twirled her hair, got up to get a

"I always take the lunch hour to do my cold calling."

napkin, and returned to the table. "You know, it's funny you asked," she said. "Now that I think of it, I happen to know that Pat Jones is having a hard time understanding hedge funds — is that what they are called? — and why the fees are so high. Would it be OK if I set up lunch with you, Pat, and me, and we can talk about that?" I am protecting identities here, but "Pat Jones" is one of the most accomplished tennis players of all time. Frank promptly replied, "No, thanks, I always take the lunch hour to do my cold calling." That's a joke, of course.

Two weeks later, Frank, his composer, and Pat Jones sat down at Pat's resplendent home, ate lunch, and Focinared. What did Frank start to do perfectly just after a low-key but resounding introduction by the composer? He told stories about his tennis career, the nightmare of living on the road, never being able to trust anyone on the business side, the pressures to perform. He spoke of the day he had a vision to help other professionals with their financial decisions, and how that prompted him to earn an MBA. The composer chimed in with the story about how Frank had been so helpful with her mom. Frank circled back with a simple but gripping explanation about how "alternative investments" (hedge funds) are important to the portfolios of high-net-worth clients, but that the fees must be understood because of the complexity of the product. Pat's jaw started to drop. Her body language sent a clear signal of relief: Somebody finally understands my pain! On the spot, Frank was awarded a sizable sum to manage.

The typical persuasion professional would be delighted with this win. Not Frank. He had the wherewithal, the fociZen, to deploy the Fisher/Dwyer method at the end of the event, too, trusting this strategy to deliver more. The response? After walking into her home office and returning with a yellow pad and a pen, Pat wrote down the names of five other professional athletes, with a full paragraph of information on each one of them. Their interests, where they live, how Frank should approach them, and so forth. Pat also said she would call all of them the following week to introduce Frank, which she did. And after several more focused touches, or interactions, with Pat, Frank won nearly all of the business. What's more, he soon counted as clients three of the five other professional athletes he had met through Pat. Frank's business continues to thrive. He is darn near Seattle in his Funk-Adjusted Returns, playing as much tennis as he wants with some of the world's elite athletes, whom he considers friends as well as clients. By the way, Frank's composer could not have been more thrilled for his success, and she was fully acknowledged for her efforts with a personal letter of thanks.

Ethnic focinarkets offer powerful opportunities, too. Blake does a great job at managing the personal finances of African American professional baseball players. He played some pro baseball himself and is African American. At his firm, he has teamed up with another advisor who focuses on Hispanic players. They are a powerful duo. But Blake wanted to find a way to expand his business and was willing to try Fisher/Dwyer. He invited one of his clients, a 22-year-old right-hander who can throw a baseball 97 miles

The world basically and fundamentally is constituted on the basis of harmony. Everything works in cooperation with something else.

Preston Bradley

per hour, to dinner, and both wives came along. The client was really pleased with how Blake had walked him through the daunting draft process, so the timing could not have been better. Halfway through the evening, Blake casually asked his player, "Do you have any suggestions for me on how I can better grow my business with other young pro ball players?" The player's wife, a latent composer, spoke up first: "Blake, you shouldn't just be working with professional baseball players. You should be working with NBA guys, too."

Don't wait for someone to take you under their wing. Find a good wing and climb up underneath it.

Frank C. Bucaro

"How do you suggest I do that, Jillian?" Blake said.

"That's easy, Blake. I'll call Don and set up a lunch for you."

"Who is Don?"

"He is an agent in the NBA. He is a phone call away from Shaq and Kobe and a lot of the big shots."

You just never know what is going to happen with Fisher/Dwyer. Who could have dreamed that the wife of the client held the keys! Thank goodness she wasn't in the ladies room at the restaurant when Blake asked the question.

I was invited along to the lunch with Don. Blake, Don, and I had a "life giving" conversation for Blake's business. I introduced Blake with some stories about how he has earned such an excellent reputation working with young pro baseball players. Blake then stepped up and started the waltz with anecdotes about how he works with young African American athletes who have come into sudden wealth with substantial contracts. He spoke about how he immediately goes to the mother of the athlete and conducts a little workshop about how life is going to change for everyone in the family. He later explained how he would provide a specific plan and financial budget for the player. I was watching Don closely. He was spellbound. After an engaging 90 minutes on the problems facing these young guys coming into such money, Don was clearly won over.

What did Blake do with perfect execution at that critical point? You got it: He asked for Don's advice on how to get started working with young NBA players. The result? "Call me next Tuesday. I have two guys I want you to meet." Focinar time, African American style! Blake was suddenly off and running in the National Basketball Association.

An important point: I reminded Blake to keep Jillian fully apprised of what had taken place. It is critical to keep your composers aware of your developments. She could not have been more overjoyed at her contribution to Blake's success. When your composers share in your success, it keeps them in the game. They continue thinking about how they can help! Jillian went on to introduce Blake to another pro baseball player — she's a gift that keeps on giving! Who would have thought it?

Or consider Jeff, a financial advisor whose focinarket is Microsoft employees. He loves the company and has grown with it. More precisely, he loves the people who work for Microsoft and is committed to helping them achieve retirements that are full of dignity. He knows the machinations, the "ins and outs," of the software giant as well as many of the employees do. Of his 160 clients, 135 work for Microsoft. He recognizes the parlance of the executives and can speak it. Call that *focinese*. He is completely plugged in to their concerns and dominates the marketplace with joy.

Jeff's Focinars are legendary. His pitch, his value proposition, his *focisition*, is completely customized to his group. It's all about them. He does not take on many new clients — he's only got room for 160; after that he is simply pruning his book of business. His clients all fly first class. How appropriate for our working metaphor that he resides in Seattle! By the way, Jeff is the second-most successful financial advisor at Ameriprise, out of 10,000. But I am convinced his F.A.R. rating is #1 in the firm.

Let's also glimpse at Conrad, another wildly successful financial planner. Conrad is from Puerto Rico, and he has formed his personal market in Central Florida around his beloved homeland. If you are a Puerto Rican doctor who practices in greater Central Florida, you most likely work with Conrad. You would be crazy not to work with him. He is the former president of the Hispanic Chamber of Commerce for Orlando and has become a master at providing solutions to the number one business concern facing M.D.s — asset protection. Not surprisingly, his practice is extraordinary.

Another example: Michael, a brilliant and dynamic accountant from Brooklyn, built a substantial portion of his business with sales executives from the financial services industry, like me. I coached him on the Fisher/Dwyer method, and shazam, he put the approach to work on me. Here is how the conversation went some two years ago, just after Michael had made my life better with guidance on re-financing my home:

Michael: "John, do you have any advice for me on how I can better grow my

A man can succeed at almost anything for which he has unlimited enthusiasm.

Charles Schwab

practice with other sales execs from the financial services field?"

John (after the big pause): "Michael, I'll tell you what we are going to do to grow your business. On your next trip to Florida, I will invite several of my colleagues out for golf. You'll join us, of course, and then we'll all have dinner. I will be sure to mention a story or two about how you've been so helpful to me personally."

Knowledge of your personal market is how you will punch your ticket in the future.

Voila! Focinar. (Feel free not to believe this story, but I promise I was unaware that Michael was practicing the Fisher/Dwyer method, until later.)

Boom, Michael was off and running in a focused market. Whenever he calls me now, he is full of information and questions related to my profession. "How is your High Yield Municipal Muni Portfolio performing in this environment of rising rates? Are you aware that your 50-ton vehicle can be taken as a write off? Do you have your 401(k) properly balanced?" I love it because he is speaking my language. And here is the kicker: I pay him a premium.

That's right: I am willing to pay extra for the customized attention. That's what happens in a personalized marketplace — people pay extra! It's the beauty of being de-commoditized. Remember: Knowledge of your personal market is how you will punch your ticket in the future.

Here are some examples of unusual focinarkets. I have seen them reap many rewards over the years:

- Rock Stars (they have "Rockinars")
- Caribbean bankers
- Widows
- South Beach (Miami) night club owners
- Episcopalian rectors
- Arcadia Rodeo Board of Directors
- NASA engineers
- Pistachio growers in California
- Motor cross champions
- Realtors in the Florida Keys
- French business execs in Sarasota
- Kentucky Fried Chicken executives

My client Sean has an amusing focinarket: affluent single women living in Wichita. Sean has tremendous functional emotional intelligence. He is a burly, John Wayne type. Chicks dig him, not in a Brad Pitt way, but in a more avuncular manner, like a woman adoring her favorite uncle. Sean dispenses financial confidence and good nights of sleep to members of the opposite sex. Many of his clients are distrustful of men, even manorexic, as one gal claims. He is the soother. As a financial advisor, he is becoming extraordinarily successful. And, of course, he began to hit the heights by using the Fisher/Dwyer method — by asking his composer for help.

After a portfolio review with Betty Sue, Sean threw out two questions. The first made clear that he is empathic, that he cares about his client: "Do you fully understand what I have just shown you and the financial plan we are going to execute? — and don't fib to me because I will be able to tell by what you do with your eyes." Betty Sue responded, "This just fantastic. I can't tell you how much better I feel." Sean's second question laid bare his respect for Betty Sue, his sense of humor, and his desire to build his business with the help of a satisfied client: "Also, Betty Sue, I have enjoyed our relationship immensely and really love working with attractive, affluent single women out here in Wichita. Do you have any suggestions for me as to how I can grow my business with more folks just like you?" After an extended 6 Mississippi count, she said, "I am going to give this a lot of serious thought." Well, three months went by, and then the phone rang in Sean's office. Betty-Sue said, "Be out here in two weeks. I have formed a ladies club for you — we are widows, divorcees, and single gals — and we are going to meet for lunch with you semi-annually to talk about finances. From now on, we are your *Wichita Chicks*." Semi-annual Focinars with single affluent ladies in Wichita! You gotta love it. When your focinarket gives itself an identity for you, great things are in order.

There's more to this story. Betty Sue introduced Sean to a woman who had just lost her husband in a tragic automobile accident. After a strong introduction by Betty Sue, Sean won the chance to compete for Jennifer's business. His competitor was formidable, a financial advisor who had been in the business 10 years longer than Sean and who had more credentials. What's more, he charged less than Sean. Yet, after describing the financial services he could provide, and does, for single women, Sean then had Jennifer attend one of the Wichita Chicks' luncheons. Soon he won Jennifer's business — and more. Invited over to the home of Jennifer's grandfather for an extended-family barbecue, Sean learned from the grandfather, "All I needed to hear was that Betty-Sue was happy with you, so take good care of my grand-daughter. Also,

When your focinarket gives itself an identity for you, great things are in order.

I plan on selling my business in the next year. A lot of these women at this barbecue will be coming into money. OK with you if we meet sometime to discuss this?" Said Sean, in between sips of delicious sweet tea, "I think I'd be able to find the time."

It's all about the *Funk-Adjusted Return.*

Gary Gould
National Director,
MetLife
Retirement

My dry cleaner has a personal market that is geographical — just a few square miles. He knows our names, comes to the house for personal pick-up, and consistently asks for guidance on how to win over others in the neighborhood. Casual, in-formal Focinars happen on our cul-de-sac. He is a part of our lives, and yes, we pay extra, gladly. In essence, the product is the dry cleaner; the dry cleaning is incidental. I would wager a substantial sum that he does not suffer from alarm clock paralysis — he appears to love what he does.

There are untold numbers of such focinarkets. And each group will have its own personal problems that need solving. That's your opportunity.

If you do not yet have a focused market, find one. Take it seriously and be clear-eyed. "Beware," as Eno Putain put it, "of inspirations that take wing on the vapors of your second martini." This is serious stuff. You should be able to visualize a real opportunity in the market — some opening so glaring that you could drive a truck through it. But only you could drive that truck. You are limited only by your imagination. Have the mind of Jack Welch, and the spirit of a Leonardo da Vinci.

Sometimes identifying your focinarket will seem difficult, I admit. But often it's easier than you think. Follow your instincts. A lot will catch your eye, but it's the niche that captures your heart that matters. Like Frank did with his tennis, focus on your passion. Perhaps your clientele is a fixed group of folks, like doctors. For example, let's say your clients are all neurologists. Perhaps one of your passions is fly-fishing. Find the neurologists who love fly-fishing and build your business on the water. That little maneuver alone will help your F.A.R. metric go far.

It might help to write out a S.W.O.T. analysis of your designs — balancing out the Strengths, Weaknesses, Opportunities, and Threats of the plan. Is there a barrier to entry for your slot? How competitive is it? Is it exciting? After completing your analysis, take it to your composers, the 10 people on your list. Stir their imaginations. Maybe they will shine a light on an unusual marketplace just waiting for you.

Section 4

"Discipline yourself and others won't need to."

John Wooden

Former basketball coach at 10-time NCAA champion UCLA

To make the Fisher/Dwyer method work for you — to maximize your Funk-Adjusted Returns — you must, I repeat must, learn how to execute a successful Focinar. In essence, you must master *focinology*, the study of all that goes into successful Focinars. The keys are the following 12 focused initiatives. I like to call them *focatives*.

If it's free, it's advice, if you pay for it, it's counseling.

Jack Adams

1. Let your composers lead the way

The Focinar must be born out of the imagination of one of your 10 best clients, your composers. Remember that, because most of my clients get lost on this critical tenet. Take a serious look at your composers. Again, you love them, and they love you. But would you be willing to exchange stations with them in life? That's right: Do not bother asking for advice from someone you would not switch places with. Generally speaking, the Fisher/Dwyer method should be used only with those for whom you have immense respect. Your treasured composers are the perfect candidates. Just like you wouldn't care in the least about advice from that knucklehead client, conversely, you should be thirsting for advice from your treasured composers.

The challenge is to engage them in a way that may seem unnatural. Most persuasion executives are Type A personalities. This means we love to control stuff. But that can be fatal when using Fisher/Dwyer with your composers. You simply must be disciplined and avoid trying to control your composer's response to Fisher/Dwyer, to a request for advice. There is too much hanging in the balance. Discipline. Discipline. Discipline. Welcome it and wear it like your favorite belt. The composer holds the keys, not you. Allow her the space to create a plan. At first, your question may throw her off guard. She may turn her head somewhat sideways and glance out the window quizzically when you request her advice. Let her imagine. The mojo is brewing, and when she responds, you will have the chance to learn something immensely valuable.

Believe me: You will not elicit help from your composers unless you fight off the Zero Sum Monster that lives in all human beings. When we have an encounter with another person, we tend to think it is a win-OR-lose situation. Let's say you and I want the same orange. We haggle. We posture by pretending we don't want the orange all that much. What would typically happen? Ultimately, we are likely to cut the orange into equal parts and go about our business. "Well, I didn't get screwed," we might think to ourselves as we walk away. The Zero Sum Monster might be whispering to us, "There was really only a 50 percent take for each of us." Yeah, but what if each party had discovered that both actually had different interests? That he uses the peel for fertilizer; that I need the juice to sell to grocery stores? Eureka! We could strike a deal in which we each get 100 percent of what we need from the one orange. The monster is slain. This, in a sense, is what you can accomplish with the Fisher/Dwyer method. You are doing due diligence and potentially allowing for a breakout mutual gain.

Ask yourself: In a world in which most of us couldn't be faulted for thinking we have Attention Deficit Disorder, what kind of marketing turns us on? Do we want more mail, snail or electronic? Do we want a cold call? Do we want to attend a seminar conducted by a stranger? *Heck no*! We want to hear from our friends that "so-and-so is who you need for your financial services, real estate needs, insurance needs, interior design needs," and so on. That is an inescapable reality today. As a business development officer, for instance, no longer can you just plop an ad in the yellow pages and wait for stuff to happen. So if you accept that premise, the central question behind successful marketing defaults to, "How do I get my composers (10 or 20 or 30 of them) to talk me up?" It is

The best way to understand people is to listen to them.

Ralph Nichols

essential that you learn how to earn 100 percent of the orange when talking with these folks.

After posing the question for advice on how best to grow your business "with other folks just like you, Sally," promptly shut your mouth. DO NOT SPEAK. For you Type As, this will be painful. But when your composer hears you, and fully digests your request, the heavens just might open. I know this runs contrary to so much that you've been taught. Remember the "always be closing" mantra? I remember vividly having to endure, early in my career, the prattle of some jarhead sales consultant who just loved displaying an enormous gold medallion that dangled in his exposed chest hair. He would drivel on about how "you gotta be closing the deal from handshake-hello to handshake good-bye." Pukeville.

A Focinar is not about closing ANYTHING. It's about OPENING more desirable accounts. It's about opening meaningful relationships, and you get there by giving your composers an opening.

Behind a Successful Focinar

Lisa Grant, a colleague who handles New York City for American Century, suggested to Paul, a big-time bank client, that he try the Fisher/Dwyer method with one of his customers. Paul was understandably skeptical. His customer had not offered up a referral in the seven years Paul had worked with her. But Paul went ahead, figuring he had nothing to lose. Worst case, he figured he would be complimenting his client. Paul tried Fisher/Dwyer during a portfolio review.

Paul: "Sarah, I love working with you. You are one of my favorite clients. I'd like to work with other successful business people in Manhattan like you. Do you think it's a good idea?"

Sarah: "Yes."

Paul: "Great. If you were me, how would you go about doing it? Do you have any advice for me?"

LONG PAUSE

Sarah: "I'm not sure, but let me think about it."

Paul was disappointed, thinking Sarah would once again fail to give him any leads. A week later, however, Paul received a phone call that completely validated his use of the Fisher/Dwyer method. The caller, whom he had never spoken to before, said, "Paul, you don't know me, but I'm John. I'm a friend of Sarah's. Not only is she a great friend of mine, but she is the smartest person I know. She told me you are great at what you do and that I should give you a call." After interviewing him, Paul found out that John sat on the board of directors of one of the oldest and most prestigious hospitals in Manhattan. In addition, John had patents on medical technology that made him the ideal, high-net-worth client Paul was looking for.

"I need help, Paul," John said. "I have about $25 million in liquid, investable assets that I need to put somewhere, but I don't know what to do. I'm already sold on working with you because of Sarah's endorsement, but I just need to figure out what my next move is. Can you help me?"

Paul was floored by how easy it was to execute the Fisher/Dwyer advice process — and wonderfully surprised by its immediate results. His long wait for a referral from Sarah ended as soon as he embraced Fisher/Dwyer, gave his composer an opening, and let her lead the way.

Listen to Brian, one of my best pupils and an enormously successful investment manager, share another great story about giving his composer the space to help Brian boost his business. Naturally, Brian's entreaties led to an outstanding Focinar.

"I said to Joe, 'I really want to build my business with other successful executives from your organization. What should I be doing?' All of a sudden time stood still. My mouth went dry. The silence was deafening. I wanted so badly to talk, to make suggestions. I started tapping my foot to relieve stress. Finally, after a tortuous 5 Mississippi count, he responded, 'The first thing you are going to do is come to my board meeting, and we'll explain why your 401(k) retirement plan is so compelling.

The second thing you are going to do is stop playing footsie under this table or else you'll be getting a punch in the nose.' "

After he realized Joe was only joking, Brian won the major firm's retirement plan when he successfully conducted a Focinar at Joe's board meeting. Brian's Funk-Adjusted Return soon started zooming from Atlanta to Kansas City — "chrome wheels, fuel injected, and stepping out over the line." Like Bruce Springsteen said, Brian was "born to run." Cheyenne was coming fast, as Brian realized he was now in a position to jettison a number of knucklehead clients.

Firing a client may seem pointless, but I assure you it's just the opposite. Donald Barden, a Managing Director at MassMutual Retirement Services, learned this lesson about a decade ago. Don was working in a small town in Georgia when he met an older insurance salesman who looked as if he had stepped off the set of Matlock. He had gray hair and wore a seersucker suit with a bow tie. Yet his

When you seek advice, do not withold any facts from the person whose advice you seek.

Abu Bakr

crusty comportment belied his success, both material and otherwise. He was eccentric but genuinely happy.

During a seminar, the man explained to Don—in an amazing bit of wisdom—that how much time you spend with your most profitable clients is the ultimate key to how much success and joy you get from your career.

Soon after talking with this fellow, Don came back to his office and immediately wrote down the names of the clients who took up most of his time and energy. He then had his assistant do the same thing without looking at his list. Later, they compared notes and found that both of them spent the vast majority of their time (somewhere near 80 percent) bogged down with the same 10 clients! He then compared their list to the revenue these clients generated, and to his surprise, they accounted for only 10 percent of his income. So 80 percent of Don's day was spent on clients who generated only 10 percent of his firm's revenues. He soon realized what must be done. He immediately sent those 10 clients a termination letter, notifying them that he would no longer provide service after 30 days. He would assist them in finding a new broker, but in the end, he was firing all of them.

The happy result: Don soon tripled his production and revenue. By clearing up 80 percent of his time he found he could now devote the bulk of his energy to his best clients, the ones who generated the most revenue. Cleaning up his book of business was incredibly worthwhile, professionally and personally. Not surprisingly, his Funk-Adjusted Returns began to soar.

Today, Don is fond of saying you should work only on the things that are most important and most productive to your mission. I am sure many of your clients don't fit this description. Who does? Your composers.

Let me be clear here: There is no better feeling in business than to be in a position where you can jettison bonehead clients. It is fantastically joyful, comparable to sex or a buzzer-beating tomahawk dunk to win a basketball game. You get there by letting your composers lead the way.

2. Get the timing right

As wondrously effective as the Fisher/Dwyer method can be, it will not work if your timing is wanting. The best time to execute Fisher/Dwyer is just after you have made one of your composers' lives better, particularly in a material fashion. Robert B. Cialdini, PhD, a professor of social psychology at Arizona State University and an international authority on persuasion, teaches about the significance of "moments of power" between individuals. For example, just after a client offers you a heartfelt thank-you for a thoughtful service, or after you sense that you have made a noteworthy contribution to the individual's life, it's a "power moment." And it's precisely when the Fisher-Dwyer method should be deployed.

Some may call this the law of reciprocity. That is, nature does not like disequilibrium. This holds true in relationships as well.

Let's say my child suddenly falls ill with a rash, and I take him to the doctor's office. After an assiduous workup, the doctor diagnoses my child and dispenses the appropriate medication on the spot. Suddenly my child shows signs of improvement. The rash disappears in front of my eyes. I am beyond thrilled — and I have a strong desire to make things even with the doctor. Now, imagine the doc is interested in growing his practice; managed care has socked it to his business model. What would happen if he casually and genuinely posed a simple question to me, like, "John, I am new to Winter Park, and I would really like to grow my practice with other young professionals like yourself. Do you have any advice for me?" Of course I know just what to say. "You better believe it, Doc. Grab a staff member and sit down for a moment. I will introduce you to the following 20 families. Here are their addresses. In fact, I am having a barbecue this Saturday. Why don't you come by, and I will introduce you to many of them?" Focinar City. It is important to note that the success of the doctor's practice, had I not been prompted by the Fisher/Dwyer process, would have been the last thing on my mind.

Some of you may read this example and say, "Yeah, but the doctor just isn't going to do that. He's got too much pride." To which I reply, unequivocally, "Pride is a very, very bad thing." In fact, pride is the antithesis of a successful Focinar. The terrible thing about pride in the business development process (and relationships in general) is that it squelches what could have been. It's a silent killer in the human experience. But humility and strength (empathy and assertion) often serve wondrously, setting the table for discovery, like the creation of the Wichita Chicks. If you want to change your results, you must find the humility and the strength of conviction to alter your behavior.

A humble person is totally different from a person who cannot recognize and appreciate himself as part of this world's marvels.

Rabino Nilton Bonder

And, remember, no matter how much humility and strength you muster, you won't capitalize on them unless you get the timing right. You have a window of time to ask for advice that is the most opportune. It's a moment of power, as Dr. Cialdini would say. (Some people would say there is leverage here. For the record, this book will not use the word "leverage" when discussing human affairs. The word should be reserved for the turning of the wrench. As I recall, Enron executives routinely used the word in describing business deals.) If the doctor asks me about his business six months after he heals my child, the question would lose some of its power. I would not be inclined to respond with such zeal.

To those of you who are thinking that this approach is manipulative, and not genuine, I say hooey. Think of a business (or personal) relationship you treasure. Maybe it's with your hairdresser, priest, weight trainer, whatever. Now, imagine the joy you experience when you introduce this person to a prospective client. It may seem fleeting at first. But with joy, what it lacks in length, it makes up for in height. It feels great, and everybody wins. In fact, Focinars do wonders to fortify relationships of all varieties. I have not seen one at which any party has felt manipulated.

3. Pick the place

It has been my experience that the Fisher/Dwyer method should be executed in an ideal setting — someplace casual, comfortable, and unthreatening. My clients, mostly financial service professionals and accountants, often meet at someplace hip, like Starbucks. Why is this significant? It is all about your composer and his comfort level. You want him to feel perfectly relaxed when you ask for advice. If you typically wear a tie, loosen it. This is a casual conversation with someone you have genuine affection for. You want your composer to speak from the heart when he responds to your request for advice.

Setting is just as important when it comes time for your Focinar. While the location must be born out of the imagination of your composer, you may want to weigh in on some of the details to get the setting right. But you have to be gentle. Suggestions that begin with the words, “It’s been my experience…” are always helpful. I once participated in a Focinar in Arcadia, the oldest rodeo in Florida. The location certainly matched the interests of the attendees. They were almost exclusively ranchers. But we could hardly communicate because of the public address system. Something was lost. The setting matters — and the ideal setting is a prelude to success.

4. Put a premium on introductions

As a persuasion executive, you want personal introductions. Referrals are infinitely weaker, more diluted. My position is that asking for referrals is fine, but that such a request is not nearly as powerful as the Fisher/Dwyer method. In fact, in the financial services industry, asking for referrals can actually be harmful. If you ask your best client for referrals, he might be a little put-out. He might not want his best friend or neighbor to have the same financial advisor because the neighbor might learn of his financial status. That could be awkward. I don’t know exactly why, but asking for referrals just doesn't elicit magic the way Fisher/Dwyer can.

An introduction born out of the Fisher/Dwyer method can involve a seismic shift. It can be life-changing. After the introduction, you will become the focinator, working in concert with your composer toward a successful Focinar.

The best introductions have two parts, the informal and the formal. The informal is the "tee up." This is where you begin to shine in the eyes of others, gaining sacred ground. The platform is being constructed. Your composer says something to his friends like, "You have just got to meet this guy, Harvey. He's the most brilliant and unknown attorney in Jacksonville. He is young and hungry, with reasonable fees, and he made all the difference for my wife and me, making some very complex matters easy to understand. And I think he graduated Summa Cum Laude." From then on, you will appear to be a shining light to your composer's friends, as opposed to just any other attorney. That is exactly where you want to be when the Focinar takes place: up on higher ground, shining, with a brilliant value proposition to deliver. Too often, or rather, practically always, the "tee-up" is given short shrift by persuasion professionals — they gloss over the intricacies and implications. A good "tee up" creates a platform from which a persuasion executive can exert her authority. So make sure your composer has all the critical information he needs for you to shine during the "tee up" —

your credentials, accomplishments, and perhaps bits and pieces that would make a great story about you. With this information, your composer will have no trouble delivering the formal introduction at the Focinar. I know it may feel a little self-serving to tell your composer how great you are, but he will more than likely appreciate it. After all, it will make his job of teeing you up and introducing you that much easier.

I have worked with a smart, young independent wealth manager who is in charge of a staggering sum of money for his age. The sum is growing voluminously because he landed a prominent executive banker as a client and the banker happens to be one of the world's greatest composers. When the banker tees-up this advisor, four out of five times the ensuing introduction leads to the opening of a major account. It is a glorious process. The banker will say with enthusiasm to his cherry-picked acquaintances, "I want you to gather your financial statements and go see Joe. He studied finance at Wharton, is honest as the day is long, and has saved me a truck-load with his sophisticated tax harvesting and structured portfolio strategies." Boom — the business starts flowing to Joe like a beautiful mountain stream. As I write, deals are happening for Joe with high-quality clients.

To the extent possible, pay attention to what your composers say about you in tee-ups. The Harvard Business Review talks about the 360-degree self-assessment strategy: You are continuously gathering knowledge from all directions on the perceptions you are generating. When speaking on your behalf, a composer should hit on your strengths and on what you can accomplish for potential clients. Stories are best for the latter. I have a client who asks quite directly how her composers tee her up. She looks for trends in the perceptions of how she conducts business. She gets a clear view of how her composers feel about her strengths and weaknesses. This is vital information. Having this data will ensure that what she says she does and what the composer says she does are congruent. This is the "echo effect." Congruent messaging to the attendees at your Focinars is essential.

Dr. Fisher says that the number one impediment stopping executives from advancing is their inability to become aware of how they are affecting others. We are too busy paying attention to our own thoughts to be aware of our impact. A successful persuasion executive will make every effort to understand how she is being perceived.

When the time comes for a formal introduction, make it easy for your composer by writing out suggested language that reflects what you want your attendees to know about you. This is critical. Remember, introductions are magic for your business development. I have no science on the following claim, but after 15 years of professional persuasion, I can say with utmost confidence that the quality of a composer's introduction is directly proportional to the velocity with which you will sign up new clients from the ranks of those attending your Focinars.

Think back on your life, and I bet that most of the positive turns hinged on introductions. Every one of my professional positions started with an introduction. How did you meet your spouse, incidentally? I wonder what the composer said about you in that tee-up?

The quality of a composer's introduction is directly proportional to the velocity with which you'll sign up the prospect.

Institute of Focinology

5. Respect and connect with your audience

When your first Focinar is a go, it is critical that you treat your attendees with utmost respect — and bond with them. All too often the speaker (or would-be focinator) just stands up and starts blabbing. A prime chance is lost. Just after the introduction is completed and you step up to the microphone,
I want you to pause for at least a 3 Mississippi count. Call this
a focused pause — a focinause, if you will. Make eye contact with your attendees — your focinees; create some subtle tension.

This is a perfect time to button your jacket, sending a message of earnestness. You are now in charge — make that clear. And when the composer hands you the floor, be ready to make some good music.

A Focinar should be intimate, just like Jesus with his 12 Apostles. To facilitate intimacy, keep your attendee level to no more than 20. You are working to bust out of the commoditization racket we all find ourselves in. Your attendees need to have a feeling of intimacy. It breeds connection.

The Focinar is about the focinees — about getting their problems solved. You want them to feel connected. A room filled with 100 people is hardly intimate. People talk among themselves, doodle, daydream, whatever. At your Focinar, you want focinees who are engaged in the subject matter. When there are no more than 20, the intimacy gives them a chance to engage.

What's more, and this is huge, so I am going to shout it: GET THEM TALKING. Maybe your focinees will be contentious and feisty — how perfect. Robert Mnookin, J.D., a professor of law at Harvard University, speaks of the necessity to waltz between empathy and assertion when making a presentation. Empathy and assertion are cousins to the two qualities I wish for my children: humility and strength. Dial in to your focinees' issues, body language, and mood, and acknowledge these feelings. Demonstrate your knowledge of their particular funk. Then, on your call at the line of scrimmage, act like a quarterback with your personalized value proposition and make a bold play. Assert. Get radical. If they sense you are genuinely in tune with their concerns, you will be free to be as colorful, forceful, and energetic as your imagination allows. This is power.

President George W. Bush had a breakout leadership moment when he grabbed the bullhorn and spoke to the free world the day after the 9/11 catastrophe. His dance between empathy and assertion was superb. "I hear you. America hears you. The world hears you (empathy)… Justice will be served (assertion)." He was not scripted. Again, NOT SCRIPTED. As a focinator, you should not be scripted. If you cannot perform without a script, you have not worked hard enough at your material — you are pre-focinated. Roll up your sleeves and get to work. Envision yourself as a duck gliding on a pond. You appear efficient, seamless, completely graceful. Yet under the water, entirely out of view, you are paddling frenetically — working with abandon.

Winston Churchill, one of the greatest figures of the 20th century, understood the value of appearing unscripted. Upon drop-off to an important speaking engagement, the Prime Minister told the cabbie to just sit still for a moment and keep the car parked momentarily. "Is there anything you need, Sir?"

said the cabbie. "No," Churchill responded, "I am just taking a moment to prepare my extemporaneous remarks."

Greg Blackwell, a senior marketing executive with Ameriprise Financial, does a remarkable job with his Focinar waltz. He works with retirees, helping them overcome their accounting and investment concerns. He is a walking, talking interpersonal just-in-time mechanism. He delivers solutions to his focinees as efficiently and effectively as possible. After he is introduced, he pauses, then says with a wry smile, "I am here to discuss your demons with respect to your financial life." Many of the silver-haired focinees chuckle. Next, he takes out a notebook and remarks, "OK, give 'em to me one at a time — tell me your most hideous fears about your finances." Typically, nobody will jump in at this point, and Greg knows it. So he tells a story. He pulls out a picture of an attractive elderly woman who is bagging groceries. "My job is to ensure that you don't have to end up like Jane here — forced to bag groceries to supplement her income because she didn't do financial planning appropriately." Something then changes in the ether of the meeting. He has just demonstrated he understands his focinees fully. There is silence in the room. The focinees now thoroughly trust him. In business, trust is numero uno — even ahead of love.

Once Greg starts delivering his material — the value proposition, or focisition, that he will use to kill those demons — his words are perfectly suited to his listeners. He invokes stories of his grandparents' struggle in the Depression. He discusses the importance of having non-callable bonds in a portfolio. For silver-haired focinees, the fear of taxation is not nearly as great as the fear of running out of money, and Greg can conquer this fear by speaking retirees' financial language — words they can understand.

It's focinese. The language of a Focinar should be focused like a laser on the concerns of the people in the audience. When Greg speaks, something starts to happen in the room. One by one, focinees start to speak up and relate their concerns. Greg feverishly captures every remark on his yellow pad, then repeats it back to them, showing he is in tune with their fears. "My son is lazy. I love him, but he's lazy. So how the hell am I going to be able to afford to send my grandchildren to college? … What's this thing called a reverse mortgage? … Should my children inherit my Roth IRA? Is Warren Buffett plotting to take over the world?" … And so on.

Section 4

Human beings do not like the sensation of not being heard — it's maddening. We simply freak out when the other party is not listening to us. In the business world, however, this conflict creates opportunities. Your competitors might not be listening to their clients as well as they should. At the Focinar, everybody who attends should end up departing with a sense that they have been heard. And even if the focinees simply grouse about their concerns, hallelujah, you've just gleaned some critical market intelligence. Now all you have to do is deliver the right remedy for these concerns, and you are going to have some new happy clients, the best kind.

A Focinar with Greg has wonderful give-and-take. It feels like an Oprah show! Oprah-nar! It's a snuggle fest. Greg's focisition (his focused value proposition) is entirely unscripted. He weaves in and out with sensible solutions for the focinees' myriad financial fears. He also unearths other issues that his focinees don't even realize they should be concerned about — call that leadership on Greg's part. When it's over, not one of the 15 to 20 focinees will walk out without feeling great about that executive named Greg.

I have witnessed Greg's composer wrap up the Focinar with a benediction of sorts, recapping the focinees' concerns and spelling out Greg's remedies. The composer reminded the focinees of the focused conclusion, the focinusion, which is to schedule a one-on-one meeting with Greg to review their financial statements. Incidentally, benedictions are a wonderful addition to the Focinar. I recommend checking with your composers to see if they think it makes sense. When performed appropriately, it's a beautiful thing.

Remember to let the spotlight shine on your composer at the event. It's his baby, after all. After his introduction, however, you need to step up with your value proposition and your active empathy. And here is more critical advice: At the Focinar, if you are able to articulate the concerns or pain of your focinees better than they themselves can, you are in an ideal spot to win the business. Hear that? Do what Greg does. Professor Fisher, of the Harvard Negotiation Project, tells me, "Articulating someone else's position better than he or she can articulate the position is vital in commanding respect and earning trust." Again, you must connect with your focinees. Articulating their concerns builds that bond.

Jack Kemp, the Republican vice president nominee in 1996, could do this magnificently. Having grown up the son of a trucker in a middle-class setting, he could passionately articulate the values of the rival Democratic Party. But then he would remind his audience that the modern Democratic Party had lost its way. His proof? "John F. Kennedy, iconic Democrat, was for less taxes, a strong military, and was a member of the National Rifle Association" — issues central to Jack Kemp's contemporary Republican Party. President Bill Clinton (along with Ronald Reagan, the two greatest persuasion executives of the last 50 years) also seems to have an innate ability to say exactly what his listener is feeling, in a manner that is supremely eloquent.

The legendary Bono, lead singer for the band U2, unmistakably understands this concept, too. While giving an interview on MSNBC about his crusade to end starvation in Africa, Bono was quick to tell Tim Russert, "This is no misty-eyed Irish rock star's foo-foo talk… We have a real plan to end suffering on this continent." He completely disarmed all of us who were prepared for some sappy entertainer's mumbo-jumbo about ending world hunger. He then commanded attention for his plans to meet with the leaders of the industrialized world and fashion a realistic plan for his cause. The point is that empathy — genuine connection — is a powerful force; please work on it. Start tonight with your spouse or child: Listen to them. Articulate their concerns. Make a connection.

6. Master the art of storytelling

Nothing is as magical as storytelling. Right after your composer gives you a resounding, customized introduction at your Focinar, the right strategy is to tell a story, just like Frank, the tennis player, did. (Hopefully, your composer told a story about you in the introduction). If you're a funny person, use humor. If you're a details person, use explicit details. Just be true to yourself as you deliver this focused anecdote, or focedote, and be passionate. This is the opening of your Focinar, and it must be gripping. Do not make the mistake of starting your focedote with a bromide such as, "Thank you, Bill, for that kind introduction. It is a real pleasure to be here tonight." Snoozeville. You're wasting everybody's time.

In his 2005 best-seller, Blink, author Malcolm Gladwell writes eloquently about instant cognition, the conclusions that people make in the "blink" of an eye after encountering someone new. He says it takes no more than two seconds for a person to jump to an incredibly powerful conclusion, one that's actually rational despite its amazing speed. The people attending your Focinar are forming an impression just that quickly when you first open your mouth, so don't blow this. Beforehand, practice your compelling opener until it truly sounds like you are speaking from the heart. Find someone who will give you candid feedback. The focedote should have some color, some real human relevance. And the theme should dovetail with your focused value proposition, or focisition.

If you're wondering when this book is going to mention Microsoft PowerPoint presentations and over-head projectors,

Forget overhead images – your eyes are the only projectors you'll ever need.

stop right now. Nothing is more damaging to your message. Presenters often hide behind these toys, to their detriment. When you use them at a Focinar, you direct your focinees' attention away from your eyeballs, the windows to your soul. This is disfocinating. It's like when you find yourself in a cool blues bar, and the bartender decides to turn on a television set. Poof — the magic disappears. Keith Ferrazzi, author of *Never Eat Alone: And Other Secrets to Success, One Relationship at a Time*, says, "The slickest PowerPoint presentation can't compete with the development of real affection and trust in capturing hearts and minds of other people."

Think back on the greatest presentation you have ever experienced — perhaps it was delivered by FDR, Lou Gehrig, JFK, Martin Luther King Jr., Ronald Reagan, or your high school football coach. The message went from his or her heart to yours, lightening-like, and you were inspired. PowerPoint images on the wall clutter this current. Especially in our era of Adult Attention Deficit Disorder, the images on the wall, irrespective of how colorful they may appear, are an opportunity for anyone's mind to scamper off. Talk about putting someone into a persistently vegetative state — there's nothing more reliably disappointing than a PowerPoint presentation! I gave them up some five years ago, and it was one of the best professional moves I ever made. I suddenly realized that the product is John Evans. Your data are incidental; show them in handouts.

Without these technological barriers, you will find it infinitely easier to re-connect should you make a misstep and lose your focination, your focused concentration. All you need do is slide back into direct visual contact with anyone in your audience. Eye contact is the river source for re-focination. The true focinator knows exactly where to return to get centered — not with the images on the wall, not down to his handout on his desk, not out the window. With practice, you'll find it soothing to realize that you

There's nothing more reliably disappointing than a PowerPoint presentation!

always have a place to get centered. Eyeball to eyeball, soul to soul, is just that place. Trust the current and your assertion (story) or empathy will return.

"Just let your love flow, like a mountain stream..."

1970s song, by Larry E. Williams

Chris runs a successful high-end workout facility, replete with wood floors and high ceilings. His focinarket is time-sensitive executives in the Orlando area whom he likes. That's right: He has defined his personal market right down to a critical subjective objective: Does he like the person or not? He actually interviews prospects — for a gym. He starts wonderfully, often in an adjoining health food store, where he opens with a story about how he was coaching a little-league team of first time players.

"In the first game of the season, Johnny made it to third base. This was the first time in his life he had stood on third base, at 6 years of age. I instructed him to run home if the next kid up to bat got a hit. Johnny said, 'OK.' Well, indeed, a line drive was struck to center field by the batter, and Johnny promptly ran from third base right into the dugout and grabbed a lemonade. Johnny thought that was 'home.' (Laughter) So my question to you, folks: When it comes to your fitness regimens, are you running toward 'home' or toward the dugout?"

This is a nice story that humanizes Chris. His focinees feast on his eye contact, and his smile serves as his garnish. His focused anecdote, or focedote, gets the focinees wondering if they are really getting the most of their workout time. His focisition then demonstrates how he caters to executives; how he employs specific stress-relief workout routines; how he keeps his routines time-sensitive; and how execs will network in his health-food store.

Chris' customized value proposition is crystal-clear to his executive focinees. They sense that he is keenly attuned to the overwhelming pressure they are under. Immediately he will then take the focinees to see the workout room. You can actually sense the delight his clientele experience in his facility. The environment, or culture, is always slightly intense, upbeat, and positive. His focisition is so compelling that he can charge a premium (a focemium!) to a collection of high-powered folks whom he really likes. The focinees believe they have hit upon much more than a gym. It's not just another (commoditized) workout room with dumbbells. Indeed, there is something in the atmosphere, and Chris knows it.

He is a master storyteller, and his practice is thriving.

7. Finish strong

At some point as you waltz between empathy and assertion during your Focinar, you will have to start to design your action step for the conclusion of the event. This is your focused conclusion, or focinusion. Focus, or intention, drives everything at your Focinar. And remember: Everything you say and do sends a message — a message that contributes to your focinees' opinion of you. You want to take them right down a funnel, through stories, dialogues, and assertions, to a focused conclusion. You must be prepared. When I take my wife out on a date, if I am ill-prepared with the destination, I will be assessing street signs, figuring out where to go, thereby misdirecting my focus from my date. The engagement will be less successful.

The focinusion should be so clear, concise, and convincing that your focinees would be foolish to do anything but act on it. They should be able to write down the focinusion on a cocktail napkin. Examples: Gather my alternative minimum tax exposure and email it to Jim (the focinator) for assessment. Tally up the dollars I have spent on vacations for my family for the last 10 years and see if it is better to own my vacations, as opposed to renting them. Take my poodle to this veterinarian who is doing innovative solutions for grown male dogs that still squat to pee. I could go on for an eternity. You must have a focused conclusion to your Focinar. The message should be clear and powerful; one your focinees will not forget.

8. Be a student of your market

In Section 3 you learned about the importance of finding your focused market, your focinarket. It's your biggest and best opportunity.

Once you identify your focinarket, I want you to become a student of that world. The knowledge of your focinarket is a sterling natural resource, an inviolable asset. Treat it that way. Too many accountants simply pick up The Wall Street Journal every day, just like every other accountant, and talk about those issues. Assign some time each day for reading information that is germane to your focinarket. That is what clients care about, after all! This kind of research improves your functional empathy, your understanding of your clients' concerns. Subscribe to what your composers and focinees subscribe to.

Get to know everything you can about the interests of your composers and focinees.

If you want to take your focused concentration, your focination, to a whole new level, you can even become well-versed on your composer's composers. That is amplified focination. Help your composers use Fisher/Dwyer with their composers, and you will achieve supernatural status. You'll become a focistar. I have a financial advisor client who teaches Focinars to his composers, many of whom are accountants quietly desperate to gather more quality clients. The advisor's results with his composers have been phenomenal, and in return he gets outstanding introductions. Everybody is headed toward Seattle in this convoy. How then can you contribute to your composers' composers?

Here's a simple idea (in fact, if this is the only thing you do after reading this book, your business will improve noticeably): Learn what magazine your composers would like to subscribe to but don't, and then go ahead and get it for them — for the rest of their lives. Every single time that magazine appears on their doorstep, they will think of you, the beloved accountant. This is marketing with a shelf-life; you can't spend money any more effectively on marketing. That's the intention of establishing a focinarket: to get your folks thinking about you, to de-commoditize your business, to win psychic real estate in perpetuity.

And here is a big takeaway: When someone knows a lot about your business and is able to demonstrate this in a compelling fashion, the perception is born that she will automatically know a lot about her business, whether she actually does or not. Do not bother to ask why. It's one of the infinite quirks of human nature, I suppose. Point is: The more you know about your clients' businesses, the more likely you are to succeed.

9. Create a culture

This is the big kahuna, the ultimate prize in your quest to compress the funk in your Funk-Adjusted Returns. Lou Gerstner, one of the most successful and admired business executives of the last 50 years, once said about business, "Culture is not the main thing. It is the only thing." Wow. That's an incredibly important insight, and entirely in lock-step with the premises of the Focinar. Your ultimate objective is to create a culture of like-minded, high-paying clients who want an experience called "you." They are thirsting to be led, and I don't care if they are the biggest of the big shots. People crave genuine direction. Remember Chris, who runs the workout facility? His clients want to be part of his vision. And that desire makes them enthusiastic about giving him guidance when he asks for advice on how to build his business.

Section 4

The importance of business culture cannot be overestimated. Examples of a particular company's culture abound, if you just pay attention. Think of the focused culture, or foculture, that you are creating as a mosaic, because everything sends a message, whether you like it or not.

A major financial services institution recently sustained a seismic fall from grace, losing tens of billions of dollars of assets because of a foul culture. I specifically recall two independent conversations I had with sales executives from the firm. I was struck by their common language. Their tone was contentious. I got the sense that these folks were instructed, explicitly and implicitly, to fight for half of the orange as they did business with clients. Both characterized their experience with clients as "hand-to-hand combat in the trenches." How disgusting. The firm deserved its substantial stumble.

On the other hand, look at Wawa convenience stores, a perfect illustration of how a solid business culture provides a competitive advantage. The convenience store business is about as commoditized as possible — buying your gas, beer, gum, and bread isn't that exciting, unless you're a pimply faced teen-ager. But Wawa, which operates over 500 stores in five eastern states, consistently posts outstanding financial results. And the company's stock has nearly doubled the return of the S&P 500 since 1977. What's more, Wawa somehow gets a couple hundred applications for each open position! What gives? The answer is culture. People, customers and employees alike, just love the place. Blogs declare, "We Love Wawa." When customers were queried as to why they love Wawa so, there was a consistent response: "The employees all seem to like each other so much." The WaWa experience is simply better.

The importance of culture, with both your employees and your clients, is paramount. Remember Jeff, the financial advisor whose focinarket is Microsoft employees? His staff is present and engaged for portions of his Focinars. He pumps them up and earnestly honors them at his events. As a result, people have a positive perception of how he runs his enterprise. Make sure you are taking care of your people, and don't be shy about showcasing your employees in Focinars and elsewhere.

Some cultures are better than others, of course, whether it be baseball teams, nation states, or businesses. The Oakland A's have been remarkably successful with minimal talent. New Zealand is a better place to grow up than Rwanda. Dell is currently a better firm than Enron was. Your Funk-Adjusted Returns are wholly dependent on your ability to create an awesome culture, populated and inspired by human beings whom you find delightful. In a sense, you could say they will become part of your family. If you can create a thriving culture, chances are you will be sitting in downtown Seattle with a hot cup of joe.

10. Practice disruption

How do you react when someone in your personal market asks you what you do? I always love to put this question to persuasion executives, and I vet the myriad responses. Candidly, they're pathetic. Rarely will someone answer the question with any passion. Nine times out of 10, I am not interested in carrying on the conversation after enduring the lame response. When you are with prospects, respond with genuine passion, no matter what your line of persuasion. Those who are able to articulate their value are more likely to be able to deliver it. Call it the *focisponse*. I am not suggesting you go over the top with some blow-hard ramble. Be true to yourself. Use fociZen, if you will. Remember: If you are not both inspired and inspiring, you will not be able to communicate your value proposition in a convincing manner. If you are passion-challenged, you might be in Miami, and perhaps it's time to change endeavors.

Sales coach Mark Magnacca, president of Insight Development Group and author of *The Product is YOU!*, specializes in helping people articulate their real value in less than 30 seconds. He has taught thousands of financial advisors to create and deliver a compelling "Elevator Speech" on the nature of their business. He rightly suggests that you respond with a question when potential clients ask what you do. This is a form of the Socratic Method.

Let's take Warren, an accountant, as an example. His Focinarket is M.D.s. When asked "The Question" at a cocktail party, he responds by saying, "You know how medical practitioners are terrified of trial attorneys?

Doc: "I hear that."

Warren: "Well, I'm a C.P.A., and I create personalized asset protection strategies that shield doctors' assets from the ravages of over-litigious trial attorneys. I am also keenly up-to-date on the S.E.C.'s position on tax shelters, so you don't have to be."

Doc: "No kidding. Who else do you work with?"

Warren: "I have plenty of clients, but my latest client, Dr. John Smith, just left me a message saying how it's nice to be able to sleep at night again. [He then tells a brief story about Dr. Smith.] Do you know Dr. Smith by chance?"

Doc: "I sure do. That's very interesting."

If you are not fired with enthusiasm, you will be fired with enthusiasm.

Vince Lombardi

Warren: "Well, I would love to talk to you about this further, at a more suitable time. Do you have any suggestions on when we might get together?" [He smoothly transitions into the Fisher/Dwyer method.]

Doc: "In fact, I am having lunch next Thursday at the club with three of my partners. Why don't you come by and join us?" [*Voila!* It's a Focinar.]

(Incidentally, Warren carries a picture of a prominent trial attorney in his wallet and will display it sometimes, if he feels the moment calls for it.)

What Warren accomplishes is focused disruption, or focinuption. Disruption has been and always will be a powerful force in the world. It can happen in a small, individual situation, like Warren's, or on a macro scale, flummoxing entire businesses or cultures. The automobile disrupted the horse carriage industry at the beginning of the last century. Microsoft disrupted IBM in more modern times. Voice Over Internet Protocol may well disrupt the gargantuan telephone industry. One of the fastest-growing firms on Madison Avenue is TBWA\CHIAT\DAY, and disruption is its forte. The firm's disruptive brand names include legends like Absolut, Apple, and Nissan.

Focinators must be disruption-minded on offense as well as defense whenever they're interacting with composers and focinees. You constantly want to be poking and prying with offense-oriented focinuption when opportunities present themselves. All the while, you want to make sure your clients are disruption-proof.

As you construct your bullet-proof (or disruption-proof) collection of clientele, you will want to give serious thought to this concept and how it affects your role. And there is no better time to execute focinuption on the individual level than when someone asks what you do. A window may just have opened — so in the words of Hulk Hogan, "Whatcha gonna do?" One of the most effective ways to disrupt somebody is by responding with a question, as Warren did.

By answering "The Question" with a question, Warren won new clients. Note that he was armed with crucial knowledge about his personal market, his focinarket. He knew doctors are freaked out about trial attorneys. He pointed out the "pebble in the shoe" of the doctor, and then told him a story that demonstrated a remedy. This scenario might look terribly simple at first blush, but I assure you that Warren put in a ton of time practicing. When you get "The Question" from someone in your personal market, you have a subtle but profound opportunity to show the prospect that you understand his pain and know how to bring relief. What is the pebble in the shoe of your personal market? Find it.

11. Reach out and touch - The pursuit of the tipping point

Vision. Focus. The top persuasion performers in any industry use these two words interchangeably, citing them as their most important tools. The funny thing is, when you employ vision to determine your natural market, focus will often just start happening. When you get introductions that were born out of the Fisher/Dwyer process, I want you to put that list of names right on the top of your desk, staring at you. Google must be employed at this stage: You should research these prospects on the Web. This is your personal market, after all! You are going to stay focused on this group for an extended period. These people will have attended one of your Focinars, received your value proposition, had the chance to be heard, and are now primed with a conclusion that you can systematically communicate to them until they are won over. And they will be won over. Have that mentality.

William Walton, president of the strategic training and coaching firm ProDirect, has some compelling research on the topic of systematic interfaces. On average, Walton finds it takes five to seven "touches" for a "highly prized" prospect to become a client. What's key, and a little surprising, however, is that the focused interface, or fociface — your communication with the prospect — should occur every 12 to 14 days for optimal results. Just go ahead and include focifaces on your calendar, making certain that each touch with the prospect is customized, that you are making some effort to remove the pebble in his shoe. After the fourth fociface, but not sooner unless prompted, I want you to assertively ask for the business. Research from the American Management Association shows that asking for the business one time, after earning trust, is optimal. Any more often and you may start to bug the prospect. Any less and you might be perceived as a wimp, ill-equipped for the task at hand.

I encourage you, too, to heed the advice of Dr. Cialdini, the professor of social psychology at Arizona State University. He recommends asking "big" when you feel you have earned the right to ask for the business. Why? Because you can always retreat. Asking for $1 million and then pulling back to $500,000 has a much greater chance of getting $500,000 from your Focinee than asking for the $500k first. What's more, you just might get the juicy $1 million response, too! If, however, you just ask for the $500,000 right at the get-go and hear a "No," you may just retreat and get zilch. My son Johnny routinely executes this focused persuasion initiative to perfection:

Johnny: "Dad, let's take a bike ride up to the courts and play tennis."

Me: "I am too tired and hungry. Tell Mommy to make me a sandwich." (This last part is a joke.)

Johnny: "OK, then. Daddy, can we please just shoot some hoops out front. I missed you this week."

Me: "All right."

Had Johnny just asked me to shoot hoops at the outset, I most likely would have barked out a "No." He retreated *within* the situation, opposed to retreating *from* the situation.

With proper execution, and proper focus on focinees' issues during follow-up, it has been my experience that more than half of these prospects will be won over. So keep that list of prospects front and center, and take copious notes of each contact as you follow up on your Focinar.

Note this sequence of touches in the quest for a highly desired prospect, crafted by an independent wealth manager named Scott. Think of this as a pursuit of a tipping point:

Touch 1: Scott meets Bo at a Focinar for "Engineers who want to Retire with Dignity." With keen empathic skills, Scott learns several things at the event about Bo — he wants a super-efficient, low-cost portfolio; he has concerns about college costs for his daughters; and he will soon be going snowboarding for the first time in his life.

Touch 2: Scott sends a thank-you note and includes information on index investing and 529 plans for college savings — the focinusion. The note is handwritten and personal, with a handwritten address on the envelope. Little things matter.

(Admit it: A handwritten note is much more desirable when you're on the receiving end than some cold, metered business correspondence.)

Touch 3: Scott drops by Bo's office unexpectedly and delivers a book on snowboarding for beginners, just before Bo's trip. His jaw drops.

Touch 4: Bo calls Scott on his return from snowboarding and wants to meet.

Touch 5: Scott meets with Bo to fully explain the efficiencies of an indexed portfolio. He tells a story about how one of Bo's colleagues has been so happy for years with his similarly devised portfolio. Also, Scott shows Bo how the 529 plan will solve the problem of college tuition inflation for Bo's daughters. They chat about snowboarding. Scott then asks for the chance to earn Bo's business. Bo's response, "Well, of course." The tipping point is reached!

"Well, of course," because Scott has focused on Bo's personal needs with a systematic, focused process that works with human beings.

12. Learn the love languages

If you take nothing from this book except this focative, you will make big gains in the business world (and personally). Dr. Gary Chapman is a nationally renowned counselor who has written a popular book entitled *The Five Love Languages*. Buy the book and read it, because the message has profound implications for your trip to Seattle. What Chapman's decades-long research indicates is that human beings have, generally speaking, five different ways in which they receive love. (Hold on: I promise this won't be too sappy.) Every person has a primary mechanism for receiving his or her *focistrokes*. "The Five Love Languages" include:

- Words of Affirmation: Mark Twain once said, "I can live for two months on a good compliment." This person has to hear words of encouragement to feel valuable.
- Quality Time: This person needs to feel your undivided attention; you have to spend meaningful time together, communicating.
- Receiving Gifts: This person responds favorably to material gestures.
- Acts of Service: Doing something for this person that you know he will appreciate. Go mow the lawn of your best client for no reason. This is my wife — when I work in the garden for her, good things often happen that evening.
- Physical Touch: Should be clear, but proceed with caution to avoid any impropriety. With this person, perhaps a hug at the conclusion of the meeting.

There are, of course, derivatives of these languages — Chapman calls them "dialects" — but all of us get our ya-yas primarily from one of these five languages.

It is critical for you to learn which language your composers speak. I want you to pay close attention to your prospects at your Focinar and subsequent meetings, looking for clues about their love language. When you can figure this out, your chances of have a lifelong, meaningful relationship skyrocket. This is the ultimate in functional empathy.

Along the way, concentrate as best you can on the plights of your composers and focinees. I want you to start thinking as they would think, feeling as they would feel. Be forthright in your meetings, probing about their greatest aspirations and greatest fears. Your empathic skills must be continually improved upon, for the rest of your life, along with your assertion skills. The nature of business going forward demands no less! As these two forces are improved upon, expect to see the blessings flow. In essence, you will have the keys to your clients' hearts — and your competitors will become "wisps of undifferentiated nothingness," as Kurt Vonnegut might say.

Section **5**

"The person who is the master of living makes little distinction between work and play, their labor and their leisure. They hardly know which is which. They simply pursue their vision of excellence and grace in whatever they do, leaving others to decide whether they are working or playing. To them they are always doing both."

Zen Quote

Conclusion

Envision a hummingbird with wings beating at an astounding frequency. The bird can fly in and out, dart to and fro, and fully engage with its environment. That is you, or will be soon, flying with your composers and the folks to whom you are introduced. You are in control, able to produce endurable gold and joy. A well-executed Focinar captures this abundant energy, enriching the lives of soon-to-be clients — and yours. The Focinar gets your career humming. It's an elegant collaboration between you and your composers. Together, you are developing a culture that is alive, fecund, mutually gainful for all involved. Each party gets 100 percent of the orange.

Show off your enthusiasm for this win-win. Enjoy your journey between assertion and empathy. Focinees will love your boldness. There is a terrible myth in the field of persuasion that the "customer is always right." Balderdash. No, he is not.

Luck — the residue of grand design.

Connie Mack

Customers like to be engaged, corrected, entertained. You are the focinator — in control by titillating and teasing and creating solutions for your focinees. Nobody likes or respects a "yes man" — how dull.

Be careful not to blithely slip back into those crusty persuasion habits you learned in some antiseptic conference room. And make no mistake, no matter how formally or informally you have been trained in your line of persuasion, you have habits. These habits must be examined on a regular basis, and this is tough. It has been my experience that most people don't learn from their experiences. Chances are, your habits could use some fine-tuning, or perhaps even an overhaul. Sales executives at American Century do an outstanding job of keeping their financial advisors on the right track. Mike Hoffman, a competitor of mine from Fidelity Investments, is superb at taking inventory to determine whether his clients have the right marketing club in their hands. Continually ask yourself the inescapable question: "How do people like to be marketed to?" That question alone should remind you that your focus should always be on your potential clients. John Maynard Keynes said, "Worldly wisdom teaches that it is better for reputation to fail conventionally than to succeed unconventionally." The focinated approach is the well-considered, unconventional marketing approach. Remember to be careful of behaviors that trigger the blasé 90/10 rule, in which 10 percent of your clients deliver 90 percent of your business. Too much hinges on your behavior for you not to seriously assess your habits. Don't be Elliot Funkhauser!

Thoroughly focus on the solutions that your focinarket needs. The late Peter Drucker, perhaps the greatest mind in business management for the last 50-plus years, argued that executives should concentrate on their contribution, not their achievement. Achievement implies the accumulation of prestige. But if you are focused on making a contribution to your focinarket, on making a meaningful and endurable impact on people's lives, then joy and fulfillment, along with the honest dollars, will be yours. Your focinees can positively sense it, feel it, when you are acting in harmony with them, finding sensible solutions to their problems. This is your focibution — your focused contribution.

I have worked with an art dealer who is revolutionizing her practices on client

... it is better for reputation to fail conventionally than to succeed unconventionally.

John Maynard Keynes

The Focination Approach is unconventional.

acquisition. She routinely executes the Fisher/Dwyer method with her best customers. As a result, she has Focinars running regularly — some customized to women who love horses, some to successful entrepreneurs who love themes of man's control over nature, some to hippie liberals who love themes of nature's control over man. When buying she is constantly thinking of these groups and what will make their lives better. She has leaders — composers — from these groups who do most of the planning and designing of the events. This is a far cry, a radical improvement, from her old stale mass-mailing initiatives and unfocinated "wine tasting" events with heaps of unqualified strangers. Joseph Stalin was once quoted as saying, "Quantity has a quality of its own." Rubbish. Look how his society turned out. My art dealer's enthusiasm for what she is doing for her small, intimate focinarkets is palpable. She is becoming a focinator par excellence in customized art distribution. I will always seek her out

Opportunity is missed by most people because it is dressed in overalls and looks like work.

Thomas A. Edison

first when looking for art because of my sense that she wants to contribute to the aesthetics of my home. And don't forget: I will pay her more for her focused attention than what the market offers.

Now that she uses the Fisher/Dwyer method, my art dealer is wholly prepared to grow her business. She knows what works. And you do, too. Plan out your 10 conversations with your composers. Preparation is key. Remember to execute Fisher/Dwyer soon after you perceive you have added value, or contributed, to their lives. Allow the glorious law of reciprocity to work fully. Take notes on their responses, and this will demonstrate that you are serious about empathy. Remember, if your composers rebuff you, there is no harm done. Asking for advice is problem-free. There is no downside.

Suppose you are a commercial insurance agent and you ask your composer about his advice for growing your business with other successful pool-building companies. If he responds by saying, "No, Joe, I do not think this is a good idea. Most pool-building owners are a nightmare to deal with, and there's a good chance you'll find yourself all wet in the deal," you reply by saying, "thank you," because now you know you need to move on to a different focinarket. Nothing lost.

One of the best political fundraisers on a national scale, Michel J. Miller, is a focinator with few equals. A big part of his modus operandi is to go to each of the major markets of the state in which his client is competing for a national office and identify composers among the many professional occupations. Then he sets up a casual meeting for coffee. For instance, in the greater Tampa area he'll gather a small-business owner, doctor, lawyer, farmer, banker, and several other raving fans of his client. He will deploy the Fisher/Dwyer advice process with each one, asking a question such as, "Do you think you could furnish a plan for our Harris for U.S. Senate Campaign to get as many successful Tampa bankers on board as possible? Katherine really needs your help." He then lets the composer go to work, orchestrating events and talking points germane to the campaign. Miller understands exactly how to marshal the resources — the people and funding — to help get national candidates elected. He knows his focinarkets intimately. As a result, nobody raises political money like Michael J. Miller.

Jon Montgomery, Executive Vice President of Business Development at CEO America, which has developed the world's first ubiquitous digital currency, is a superb focinator, too. He raises pools of capital for the enterprise. Dealing with venture capitalists and accredited investors is a tricky business — people can turn ugly in an instant. With practice, he has become masterful at employing the Fisher/Dwyer method to assemble a first-class group of investors. His focinarket is purely subjective: His composers are like a top-flight business fraternity, wildly passionate about continuing to spread the focisition to other qualified focinees. I can listen to Jon tell stories about his Focinars for hours. Each event is unique and compelling. "Focus is the key to strength," Jon told me over lunch. "As long as I stay dialed in on assembling the right kind of folks on my team, I know I will continue to realize outstanding results. These guys are creating something way bigger than what I could have imagined. I am continually humbled by their contribution and the knowledge I get to glean from their participation." Indeed. Once you use the Focinar, you just may start creating something way bigger than you could ever imagine.

The way to get started is to quit talking and begin doing.

Walt Disney

Beware of analysis paralysis when commencing your voyage. Get started. You are equal to this task. Proper arrangement and application of common sense are all it takes. Like anything, you will get better with practice. There is no better teacher than experience, and I want you in motion just as soon as you are prepared, and not a moment subsequent. Too many of my clients get caught up on the small stuff. As the expression goes, "if you've never missed an airplane, then you are spending too much time in airports." Stop spending too much time with antiquated marketing techniques. I do not have one, not one, example of a client who has regretted enacting Focinars. But I have seen hundreds of folks who are delighted with their new approach. By avoiding the old-time marketing methods, your return-on-effort will improve substantially. Call it foconomics.

If you have trouble executing the Fisher/Dwyer method, chances are you are suffering from too much pride. The intrinsic ether that is the essence of the Focinar is humility, and your focinees can smell if you have any from a mile away. If you don't have humility, find a church, spiritual leader, or little brother and get some. Pride devours the flame of the Focinar faster than a rat can devour a Cheeto.

I have found no greater satisfaction than achieving success through honest dealing and strict adherence to the view that, for you to gain, those you deal with should gain as well.

Alan Greenspan

Take pride, instead, in your contribution. As a persuasion executive, you get to be very near a phenomenon that carries existential weight: the transaction. It is a thing of beauty. In most circumstances, it is heavenly because it allows you the chance to contribute value for a market price. In all situations, there is power inherent in the process.

As a focinator, you get to be intimately involved with transactions. This automatically gives you vitality and responsibility. The Focinar allows you to get up close and personal with the contribution you are here to make.

Persuasion, by the way, is contribution. You might say that inventing the airplane and discovering penicillin (or America) are greater feats than being a great persuader. To which I will reply that there indubitably is persuasion involved in all great achievements. Columbus had to pull off quite a deal, or transaction, with Queen Isabella of Spain to make his trip happen.

Whether you like it or not, you are here in this world to persuade. Upon birth, how effective you were with your howl determined how often and how much milk you received. If you are fortunate enough to get to a point in life where you have grandchildren, you will want to be effective in persuading them and their parents to be around you with the degree of frequency that you desire. And in between these two potential bookends of life, there are inexhaustible opportunities for you to be successful (or not) with your approaches to persuasion.

I sincerely hope my destination metaphor about a trip to Seattle resonates with you. To be able to find joy in another's joy, that is the secret to happiness — and that's how you get to Seattle. I want to see you get there. I want you to maximize your Funk-Adjusted Returns. Will it happen? If you initiate humility-filled conversations with your composers, identify your own special market, and execute the 12 "focatives" in this book, I truly believe you will increase your income and improve the quality of your life.

A closing thought - One year ago I asked Charlie Stover for advice about how I could help him grow his business. He said, "I need a book with your value-added stuff." Hope you liked it Charlie.

Please email me your success stories: www.focinar.com.

P.S.: There is no need to tell your composers or your focinees about the term "Focinar." They will only become confused. Let's just make it our little secret.

Glossary

(Entries appear in order of first reference)

Focinar: a) An event at which a group of like-minded individuals gather to hear a polished sales pitch (a customized value proposition) from a persuasion executive; b) An incredibly powerful tool for business development, inspired out of the Fisher/Dwyer advice process.

Persuasion: a) The founding principle of a sales business; b) An art and science rarely taught successfully by higher institutions, connect-the-dots corporate lesson plans, or management.

Sit-and-Swivel: The worst marketing approach of all time, in which a persuasion executive looking to grow his or her business just sits around and waits for accounts from a manager or principal.

90/10 rule: a) A simple rubric that says 10 percent of a persuasion executive's clients typically deliver 90 percent of his or her business; b) an insightful rubric that says 90 percent of a persuasion executive's clients — people he or she really doesn't like — typically generate 100 percent of the funk that leads to the executive's feeling of career paralysis.

Funk-Adjusted Returns: A persuasion executive's income multiplied by the joy he or she achieves from making a contribution to the marketplace and the welfare of others.

Funk: An undesirable experience that a persuasion executive endures in order to have success, such as spending time away from family and loved ones, playing energy-sapping corporate politics, managing knucklehead colleagues who smile at the boss while barking at the administrative assistant, or slogging through start-up challenges.

Composer: a) One of a persuasion executive's best 10 clients, who composes the "symphony" of the executive's business and whose loss would hurt the executive both emotionally and financially; b) a person whom a persuasion executive can count on for advice on how to grow his or her business.

Echo Effect: Saying the same things about your merits to your focinees that your composers have said to them.

Fisher/Dwyer Method: a) a persuasion technique pioneered by professors Roger Fisher, director of the Harvard Negotiation Project, and Charles Dwyer, PhD, associate professor of philosophy and education at the University of Pennsylvania; b) used to ask for advice from a person whom a persuasion executive is trying to influence; c) the first step for a persuasion executive when he or she begins a business-building conversation with a top-10 client.

Focinarket: a) The place or space where a persuasion executive conducts business like nobody else on Earth; b) a segment of the marketplace allowing a persuasion executive to earn a life of significance; c) a segment of the marketplace that a persuasion executive loves and dominates.

FociZen: a) The unique knowledge and inspiration that a persuasion executive develops after successfully executing a Focinar; b) the trust that a persuasion executive has in the strategy of asking clients for advice on how to build his business, and the wherewithal to use the strategy at any time.

Focinese: a) The focused, empathic, culturally relevant language used by a persuasion executive while he is communicating with members of his focinarket; b) the language used by a persuasion executive that is focused like a laser on the concerns of the audience at a Focinar.

Focisition: A focused value proposition delivered by a persuasion executive and completely customized for potential clients at a Focinar.

S.W.O.T Analysis: An analysis of a persuasion executive's endeavor that balances out the Strengths, Weaknesses, Opportunities, and Threats to the plan.

Focinology: The study of all that goes into successful focinars; must be mastered to conduct a Focinar that delivers results.

Focative: One of 12 focused initiatives that must executed by a persuasion executive for a Focinar to be a successful. They include: 1) letting your composers lead the way; 2) using timing effectively; 3) picking the right location; 4) putting a premium on introductions; 5) respecting and connecting with an audience; 6) mastering the art of storytelling; 7) finishing strong; 8) being a student of a focinarket; 9) creating a culture; 10) practicing disruption; 11) reaching out to touch a focinarket; and 12) learning the Five Love Languages.

Zero Sum Monster: a) A common belief that an encounter with another person is a win-or-lose situation; b) a belief that can be countered by using the Fisher/Dwyer method.

Focinar City: The first thought that crosses the mind of a persuasion executive when told by one of his or her best clients that like-minded people will be getting together to hear how the executive can help them meet their goals

Focinator: A persuasion executive working in concert with a composer (one of his or her best clients) to execute a successful Focinar.

Focinause: a) A "3 Mississippi count" pause made by a persuasion executive after he or she is introduced at a Focinar, during which eye contact is made with the people in the audience and subtle tension is created; b) a time for a persuasion executive to button his jacket and send a message of earnestness after being introduced at a Focinar.

Focinee: A potential client or customer who attends a Focinar at the suggestion of a persuasion executive's most satisfied clients.

Pre-focinated: a) An uncomfortable state of mind among persuasion executives in which they feel compelled to script the delivery of their customized value proposition in front of potential clients; b) a purgatory that persuasion executives need to cross (by rolling up their sleeves and getting to work) before they can appear efficient, seamless, and completely graceful in front of focinees.

Focinar Waltz: A dance between empathy and assertion executed by a successful focinator.

Focinusion: An unforgettably focused, clear, and concise conclusion, delivered by a persuasion executive at a Focinar, that spells out what focinees should do next.

Amplified Focination: a) focused concentration taken to a higher level; b) when a persuasion executive helps his composers use the Fisher/Dwyer method with their composers; c) the teaching of focinology.

Focedote: a) A focused anecdote, or revealing story with human relevance, that is delivered by a persuasion executive at the start of a Focinar and that dovetails with the executive's customized value proposition; b) exactly the opposite of a bromide such as, "Thank you, Bill for that kind introduction. It is a pleasure to be here tonight."

Dis-focinate: To direct focinees' attention away from a persuasion executive's eyeballs, the windows to his or her soul, by using techniques such as a Microsoft PowerPoint presentation at a Focinar.

Focination: The focused concentration employed by a persuasion executive at a successful Focinar, often developed best by making visual contact with focinees.

Re-focination: A state of mind that a persuasion executive can regain by making eye contact with focinees after he or she loses his or her focination during a Focinar.

Focemium: The premium that a persuasion executive usually can charge after making a compelling focisition at a Focinar.

Focistar: a) A persuasion executive so focused on seeing his clients grow their businesses that he teaches them how to employ focatives, the Fisher/Dwyer method, and the Focinar; b) a persuasion executive who knows all there is to know about his clients' businesses.

Foculture: A focused culture created by a persuasion executive that feeds and supports his or her focinarket.

Focisponse: a) A well-articulated, focused response — in the form of a question — by a persuasion executive when asked what he or she does for a living; the response spells out the value the executive can provide or is providing to clients; b) the opposite of a blow-hard ramble.

Focinuption: a) A question or related disruptive response offered by a persuasion executive when asked what he or she does for a living; b) an incredibly powerful force in the business world.

Fociface: The focused interface, or communication, between a persuasion executive and a potential client that should occur every 12 to 14 days for optimal results.

Focistrokes: The good feelings a potential client gets when spoken to by a persuasion executive in the "Love Language" that most appeals to that client.

Five Love Languages: A concept popularized by Dr. Gary Chapman, a nationally renowned counselor, in which people receive love in five distinct ways: Words of affirmation, quality time, gifts, acts of service, or physical touch; it is critical for persuasion executives to learn which of these languages his or her composers speak.

Focibution: a) A persuasion executive's focused contribution to the marketplace; b) finding sensible solutions to the problems of potential clients.

Unfocinated: An adjective that describes unfocused, antiquated marketing techniques like wine-tasting events with heaps of strangers or mass-mailing initiatives.

Foconomics: A system of economic give-and-take in which a persuasion executive receives a high return by executing marketing techniques like the Focinar instead of old-time techniques that have outlived their usefulness.

Focannoying: An adjective that a persuasion executive should feel free to use when describing the innovative marketing language in The Focinar — but only after reading the book.

A professional service person's commitment and passion toward a customer is highly correlated with a firm's long term profitability.

Mark W. Johnston, Ph.D.
Alan and Sandra Gerry Professor of Marketing and Ethics
Crummer Graduate School of Business, Rollins College